ON HENRY MILLER

WRITERS ON WRITERS

JOHN BURNSIDE ⊞ **ON HENRY MILLER**

Or, How to Be

an Anarchist

PRINCETON UNIVERSITY PRESS

Princeton and Oxford

Published by Princeton University Press,
41 William Street, Princeton, New Jersey 08540

In the United Kingdom: Princeton University Press,
6 Oxford Street, Woodstock, Oxfordshire OX20 1TR

press.princeton.edu

Jacket photograph: Henry Miller © René Saint Paul /
Bridgeman Images

Excerpt from the *Tao Te Ching*, trans. Derek Lin, from
www.Taoism.net and *Tao Te Ching: Annotated & Explained*,
SkyLight Paths, 2006. Reprinted by permission.

Excerpt from "Carmel Point" by Robinson Jeffers,
in *The Collected Poems* (Stanford University Press, 2002).
Reprinted by permission of the Estate of Robinson Jeffers.

ISBN 978-0-691-16687-2

Library of Congress Control Number: 2017961232

British Library Cataloging-in-Publication Data is available

This book has been composed in Minion Pro and Myriad Pro

Printed on acid-free paper. ∞

Printed in the United States of America

10 9 8 7 6 5 4 3 2 1

⊞ *for Phill Pass*
—Be Well

◈ CONTENTS

▩ BY WAY OF A PREFACE

I was stuck. The book was almost finished, and I was trying to make a decent fist of liking it (though only to myself, for I had yet to summon up the chutzpah to show it to anyone else), but I was failing miserably. From beginning to end (though with a great big hole where the sex should be), the book I had privately titled *Henry Miller: Or, How to Be an Anarchist* was a perfectly honorable, if rather lopsided, homage to the work I most loved by a writer I mostly admired, but the whole thing was dull as ditch water. At the same time, apart from a grudging admission that Kate Millett's critique of *Sexus* in her groundbreaking study of misogyny in literature,[1] was more or less fair, most of my "appreciation" of Miller was based, like a house built on sand, on a plucky attempt to pretend that a handful of cringe-worthy passages (though by no means all) about sex were no longer relevant and could be passed over quickly. Or rather, that they were somewhat relevant, but they had already been given enough attention, to the detriment of other, more interesting and, even (in my view), more rewarding books.

Most of all, the book I was almost but not quite finishing was as unlike anything Henry Miller might have written as it was possible to be. There was no fever, no itch, no *drunkenness*— and what I had wanted from the moment I put pen to paper was to write a book, not *about* Miller, but *after* Miller (early on, I had guessed that this project was as much about me as it was about him and, taking his cue, I didn't want the book I was writing to be an analysis of his works, but a crazy and exhilarating account of how reading Miller had changed *me*). I wanted a Miller-like book. An anarchic book with its own, emergent order. A book full of digressions and passages that were genuinely surreal (as opposed to the contrived surrealism of the Surrealists, whom Miller took so wittily to task for their programmatic approach in his essay, "An Open Letter to Surrealists Everywhere."[2] A book that somehow got to the heart of Miller's single greatest achievement, which was to move from Rimbaud's first critical stage in the remaking of the governed self as artist ("I say that one must be a seer, one must make oneself a seer. The poet makes himself a seer by an immense, long, deliberate derangement of all the senses")[3] to the next step in the process, the step (all too often ignored by bohemians) in which, if the artist is disciplined enough, a new order, a new serenity, a new drunkenness, and a new detachment emerge from the chaos. Miller—who had read his Thoreau—knew that *dérèglement* in any form was only the first step in becoming a complete artist and, unlike most of the Beats and almost all of the Surrealists, he understood the need to add anarchist *discipline* (a notion that I will come to later) to the visionary imagination.

Instead, what I had written was a kind of hearty apologia for a man whose almost child-like delight in the vagaries, not of sex itself, but of how we pretend not to see and accept ourselves as sexual creatures had led to unjust persecution and censorship, followed by a seemingly justifiable decline (and if Miller had only written, say, *The Rosy Crucifixion*, that decline in interest would not have seemed *quite* so unfair). Looking back to the beginning of the project, I now had to wonder at the self-deception I had somehow mobilized when I decided that I wouldn't write about the sex books at all (not even *The Tropics*) but concentrate entirely on the work in which Miller's wisdom, humor, and elastic prose not only echo but elaborate upon the master philosophers of anarchism's long, if misunderstood, history: The work informed by Daoist thought and a spirit of serious, though never solemn, play. The work that revealed the true extent of the Air-Conditioned Nightmare (first in America and now pretty much everywhere). The work whose only controversial aspect was its being underappreciated for so long, while the notorious "sex stuff" got all the attention.

Clearly, I could never have pulled this off. No matter how insightful and daring this other Miller might be, there was always the "woman-hater" to contend with—and to try to evade this issue, even in a fairly short book—was, quite simply, cowardice. As Jeanette Winterson remarks, in a *New York Times* review of Frederick Turner's *Renegade: Henry Miller and the Making of "Tropic of Cancer"*: "There is beauty as well as hatred in *Cancer*, and it deserves its place on the shelf. Yet the central question it poses was stupidly buried under censorship in the 1930s, and gleefully swept aside in the permissiveness of the 1960s. Kate Millett asked the question in the 1970s, but the effort to ignore it is prodigious. A new round of mythmaking is ignoring it once more. The question is not art versus pornography or sexuality versus censorship or any question about achievement. The question is: Why do men revel in the degradation of women?"[4] I agreed with this observation wholeheartedly, yet here I was trying to pull off the same old trick, and skip past the most challenging aspect of Miller's work—and that, inevitably, led to the question: Just whose sins was I trying to ignore? Or rather, why had I chosen to write about Miller in the first place, when I knew that, like so many of my other literary or philosophical "heroes," he had never apologized for his misogyny but (as Heidegger did, when confronted with his Nazi history after the war) simply brushed the whole issue aside. Typically, while Heidegger and others chose silence, Miller elected to make light of his errors, shrugging off his misogynistic past, or claiming that, in many countries, he wasn't seen as sexist at all.

For example, in a newspaper interview with the *Chicago Tribune* in 1978, Miller had this to say about a critic who had, rather astutely, pointed out that the one thing he couldn't write about was "sex with love": "Yeah, it seems to be true. I was telling my 'adventures,' you might say. It wasn't the place, therefore, to dwell on love. The sex wasn't too pretty, either. But I *played up the scoundrel in myself, don't you know, because he was more interesting than the angel*" (my italics).[5] The interviewer goes on to add that Miller

doesn't seem too concerned with predictable attacks from Kate Millett and other feminists.

"This women's liberation movement is based on an antagonism toward men. In other countries I'm not called a monster. And if you read me thoroughly—the 50 books— you'll know they're not all about sex and that includes the latest, *Sextet*. Now, they may say, "Well, he's getting old." And there's some truth in that. I don't think about sex all the time. I'm not a monomaniac. But I do think it's a very important part of life, and that it's been mishandled and misunderstood in this country."

And the article continues:

In his books, sex has been handled and under-stood quite well, thank you, by his protago-nists, who take it often and anywhere—in the back of buses, under trees, in phone booths. The obvious question is, how much is report-ing and how much is fantasy?

He grins. "My books are all autobiography. I can't write about other things. Is it vanity? Maybe, but I don't think so. It's just that I think my life was so interesting, why should I go to outside material? Anyway, I would take off— exaggerate—many times. That's what a writer is. . . . He loves words, the language, and he loves to embroider. So I never feel guilty about any inaccuracies. They were done with a good heart. It's true that many people have envied my sexual activities.

(Laughter.) Sometimes I think I envy them myself."

This interview, along with many similarly lighthearted pieces in popular magazines and newspapers, is as far as Miller was prepared to go to justify his sex writings—and, as a response to Jeanette Winterson's question, it falls very far short of saying enough. However, there are three points that should be gleaned from these later interviews, if we are to understand what I believe Miller was really up to in the "sex stuff." First, he happily agrees that he cannot, and does not even try to write about "sex with love." However, he writes often, and sometimes in ways that make the reader very uncomfortable, about love of a certain kind—and this is key. Miller is, in many ways, a romantic (and we do see this side of him more often than he is credited for, see below); it is just that his subject, in *The Tropics*, *The Rosy Crucifixion*, and such works, is not romantic love so much as its inevitable corruption in a property-based society that transforms everything, including sex, into fetishized "product."

Miller's principal concern, in fact, is with what Leonard Cohen calls "the war between the man and the woman"—and this war has nothing to do with individuals. (Nor is it what we are wont to call "the battle of the sexes.") It is a result of the *enclosure* of sexuality by a property-based system (echoing earlier enclosures of land and the means of production) by way of the institution of marriage, on the one hand, and of the artificial standards of "manliness" imposed upon boys—especially on boys growing up in the Teddy Roosevelt years, as Miller did—on the other. In fact, when he does write frankly about sex, it is not what happens between the man and the woman that is important, but how that changes, or heightens, or damages the dynamic between *male* characters. And, as so often happened in his own day-to-day life, especially during the New York years, when he turned a blind eye to June's long chain of "patrons," that dynamic has more to do with money and power than with sexuality. In short, Miller is not writing about sexual love (or any kind of love at all). He is talking about marriage or marriage-like contracts—contracts in which, on a personal level, he appears to have suffered deeply, even while continuing to enter into them. (He was, in fact, married five times, his last wife being a young Japanese singer named Hoki Tokuda, who later said in an interview: "If Henry had been my grandfather, it would have been perfect. He was funny. I laughed all the time, and he liked my sense of humor."[6] She was twenty-nine; he was seventy-six;

later, she claimed that throughout the eleven years of their marriage she and Miller never once made love). It is a wonderful irony that, in his old age years, the supposed "cocksman" of legend could write, with apparent sincerity, in a letter to Hoki:

If I gave you a sleepless night, and myself as well, it was because it was one of the very rare times in my life that I had to sleep beside a woman without touching her. When dawn came I was at least able to gaze at your countenance. What a world to study, to explore, in your night face! An entirely different face than Hoki wears in her waking moments. The face of a stranger, carved out of lava, like some oceanic goddess. More mysterious with eyes closed and features sculpted out of ancestral memories. An almost barbaric look, as if you had been resurrected from some ancient city—like Ankor Wat—or the submerged ruins of Atlantis. You were ageless, lost not in sleep but in the myth of time. I shall always remember this face of sleep long after I get to know the hundred and one faces you present the world. It will be the dream face which you yourself have never seen and which I will guard as the sacred link between the ever-changing Hoki and the ever-searching Henry-San. This is my treasure and my solace.[7]

Historically, we have been taught to be repelled—a little too sanctimoniously, perhaps—by Henry Miller, pornographer and woman hater. He is the one who is supposed to disturb us. Yet when we look at his history (the brutal, joyless mother, constantly undermining both the sad, feckless husband and the unhappy son, the ugly machismo of the Roosevelt years, when "manliness" was all, the puritanical denial of pleasurable sex in the culture he was born into) there is so much material that can be brought to bear, if not to excuse, then at least to understand Miller's apparent misogyny.[8] However, what is more disturbing about Miller is the near-pathological romanticism revealed in this letter—a romanticism so profound that he even wants to know "the dream face which you yourself have never seen." This is the Miller who haunts me, the Miller who even frightens me a little. Silent, by the side of a sleeping woman who is not his lover, but his Beloved, in a scene reminiscent of Yasunari Kawabata's great novel of the "beauty-in-sadness" tradition, *The House of the Sleeping Beauties*, this romantic voyeur wants to know the woman even better than she knows herself—and yet, at the same time, he wants her face to remain "the face of a stranger," a face that is "ever-changing" in response to his "ever-searching," a face that will become more and more mysterious, the longer and more closely it is scrutinized.[9] In short, what Miller wants, like every good romantic, is the impossible. Like the Walter Raleigh of "The Silent Lover," he wants to gaze, silently, asking for nothing because nothing could ever be enough:

> I rather choose to want relief
> > Than venture the revealing;
> Where glory recommends the grief,
> > Despair distrusts the healing.
>
> Thus those desires that aim too high
> > For any mortal lover,
> When reason cannot make them die,
> > Discretion doth them cover.
>
> Yet, when discretion doth bereave
> > The plaints that they should utter,
> Then thy discretion may perceive
> > That silence is a suitor.
>
> Silence in love bewrays more woe
> > Than words, though ne'er so witty:
> A beggar that is dumb, you know,
> > May challenge double pity.
>
> Then wrong not, dearest to my heart,
> > My true, though secret, passion:
> He smarteth most that hides his smart,
> > And sues for no compassion.[10]

When I received the invitation to contribute to the Writers on Writers series, I was delighted to have an opportunity to say something about the poetry of Marianne Moore, whose work was the single main catalyst in my desire, at fifteen or so, to write poetry of my own. At that time, I took some pride in the fact that I didn't want to *become* a poet (perhaps because of my own received working-class standards of manliness, in which miners and steel-millers were king, while poets were effete scribblers in floppy hats and purple corduroy). I simply wanted to write a few decent poems and publish them, possibly under a pseudonym, in a well-regarded literary magazine. This was just one activity among many that I would have liked to pursue; others included learning *The Goldberg Variations* from beginning to end, keeping goal for the Montreal Canadiens, and finding a hitherto unknown bird species. Needless to say, I am still working on these.

It came as a surprise then that, asked which writer I had chosen, I blurted out the name: Henry Miller. That was unexpected—and yet, at the same time, it was entirely predictable. I had been thinking for some time about what it means, not to write the odd poem or two, but to *work* as a writer, trapped in a seemingly unending struggle to render unto Caesar just enough to buy an hour or two each day to sit in a narrow room and confess, to a sheet of cold white paper, the inner workings of a botched heart. Growing up, I had not intended to take up writing as a métier. In fact—as my father frequently told me, whenever I expressed an interest in anything other than manual labor or the armed forces—I knew all too well that "people like us" did not presume to "go into" the arts, where only one in a million "made it," and that one in a million came from an entirely different background from the gray, uninspiring streets of the impoverished coal and steel towns where I was attempting, despite my father's derision, to grow up as a different kind of man from the specimen he wanted me to be (tough, hard, ready for anything, devoid of trust). I didn't even try to explain to my father that I had no illusions about "making it"; I just wanted to learn piano well enough to work as an accompanist, say, or a music teacher. Even this modest ambition struck him as unrealistic, however, and in his world, to be unrealistic was not manly.

Manly. It is a word that, for a long time, was seared into my brain, just as it was for Miller, whose own father, a feckless tailor with a fondness for alcohol, was constantly being derided and humiliated for *his* unmanliness by the woman he had married. It is clear, now, that fear of unmanliness was what drove Miller to write some of the work for which he has been most criticized (and to conceal the romantic in his soul that kept him up at night, gazing at the face of a woman young enough to be his granddaughter). His great victory, however, a victory that resulted in his finest work, was to overcome that fear, and to reject the idea of manliness that had been ingrained in his psyche almost from birth. What I admire in Miller is that victory, and I continue to find his self-transformation—nothing less, in my view, than a supreme work of alchemical transmutation—both wonderfully surprising and inspiring. In fact, it is what Henry Miller made of himself, through the act of writing, that fascinates me—and when the question arises, as it must, as to what writing is for, other than entertainment, it is his exemplary transmutation that provides the basis for at least a partial justification of writing as métier. Any writer must be careful, of course, for as Miller often remarked, the social world insists on not giving writers their due, and that, sometimes deliberate, neglect can lead us to overvalue, and even aggrandize, the work (or the self) by way of compensation. Yet, as Marianne Moore notes, speaking of poetry,

> I, too, dislike it: there are things that are
> important beyond
> all this fiddle.

Reading it, however, with a perfect
    contempt for it, one
    discovers in
it after all, a place for the genuine.[11]

The genuine was exactly what Henry Miller was after, and, in its pursuit, he excoriated every instance of duplicity and fraudulence he encountered. Before The Beats arrived, before the 1960s generation set about questioning every aspect of The System, Miller was there, mocking the Emperor's new clothes and denouncing the lies and half-truths told in high places. Yet he was more than a latter-day Jeremiah, because he stayed true to his real quest—a quest born out of unmanly romanticism and an anarchist's reverence for the natural order. It took him a long time to complete that quest—in fact, it took him a long time to begin—but when he got there, in books like *The Colossus of Maroussi*, say, or *The Air-Conditioned Nightmare*, he became more than a writer. He became a sage, in the Daoist sense of the word: not good, not venerable, not saintly, but wise to the world and to himself.

This book is not intended as a literary study of Henry Miller's work. I have made no attempt to be objective, restrained, or particularly analytical. If anything, I have tried to emulate the Miller

I most value—a writer given to digression, non sequitur, rhapsody, occasional surrealism, and, most of all, shameless polemic. I have also allowed myself, in this rewriting, to do as Henry did—to make it all about me. What I mean by that could be encapsulated in the words: "this is personal," by which I mean personal in a way that is societally inappropriate, like telling the ambassador's wife what you dreamed last night (but then, what could I do? I have no gift for small talk, and the lady—a Swedish woman—seemed so human. And to be fair, it really was an interesting dream). There may be elements of lit-crit in this book, but I am sure that no one will be deceived by that: I go back to Miller when I need his advice, his example, and his insouciance; and now, at a particular juncture of my own life, I am writing about him out of *need*. What I want to know, both as reader and writer, is whether books—or even individual sentences—can help us live more rewarding lives.[12]

In short, I have allowed myself the freedom to adopt a method that my subject himself often employs, which is to talk about another writer or artist mostly as a means to reassess and think about his own condition from a new and unexpected angle—which, at certain times in our lives, we all do. Why shouldn't we? Do we only go to literature for entertainment, or do we

sometimes open a book with the hopes of finding something, however abstract, that might
help with some quotidian transition, or ordinary grief? "Rimbaud restored literature to life,"
Miller says. "I have endeavored to restore life to
literature."[13]

This book is also personal in its response to
an active (as opposed to theoretical) philosophy
that has given me a sense of order throughout my
life, just as it seems to have done for Miller. That
philosophy is primarily based on *an acceptance of
the natural order*, as it is observed *in process*. In
choosing to write about Miller, I knew immediately that I would want the piece to reflect what
I have learned from his writing (and his readings
of texts as various as the *Dao De Jing* and Rabe-
lais); I also wanted to relate his thinking directly to
my own life, both as a writer and as an embattled
specimen of humankind living in an age when
the Air-Conditioned Nightmare went global. This
personal approach may be considered suspect by
some (a case of smoke and mirrors on the part of
one who is not, and does not pretend to be, a Miller
scholar), but this choice was inevitable when I
came to write about a man who, as contrary and
sometimes reprehensible as he was, remains, to
my mind, a variety of spiritual alchemist.

At the same time, I would argue that nothing
has misdirected us more, in all our seeking after

knowledge, than a mistaken concept of "objectivity," adopted sometime in the mid-twentieth century by the Humanities from Mainstream (i.e., "hard," possibly even "manly") Science, presumably in the hope of attracting more equitable levels of research funding. I also feel that, in an age of environmental crisis, writing that does not work upon us—mind and soul and imagination alike—either by reinforcing the better angels of our nature or demanding that we change our harmful ways, *right away*, is not much more than another form of entertainment, like a sit-com, or a game show. As we have seen from the clumsy attempts of governments around the world to address climate change (mostly by giving big businesses and landowners astonishing subsidies for the least effective "solutions"), what is needed (and Miller would be the first to say so, quite unequivocally) is radical—alchemical—change in every aspect of our day-to-day lives. This change begins in a systematic unpacking of our conditioning to reveal the raw, contradictory, but ungoverned self encased in each societally engineered carapace and, with it, an inherent sense of order that transcends the industrialized culture that we now endure. There is no guarantee that a society of ungoverned individuals could, at this late stage, solve the major environmental problems we face, but we would, at least, be ready to live as truly *human* beings in what might well become an increasingly creaturely world. As with other artists, writers make something, and, if that something is to have any external moral value, we have to rely on the elegance, honesty, or even (unfashionable term) beauty of the process of making that is revealed in the finished product (essay, poem, novel, inspired scrawl of graffiti).

At the same time, the morally directed writer can insist on specific values that have an overall impact, in possibly minor but incremental ways. Like Henry Miller, we can demand that language be used to its fullest, and not in the reductive and/or euphemistic ways that the powers-that-be prefer; like Miller, we can demonstrate that a good description of anything has a value in itself; like Miller, we can insist on long, sometimes complex sentences, with their due proportion of sub-clauses and qualifiers, when the narrative situation requires them. We can apply these gifts to appreciation, as well as to critique; we can sing our connection to all other living things, and we can remember that our responsibilities to the world around us overlap precisely with our enjoyment of that world. As Goethe says, in an essay on scientific method, "As soon as we consider a phenomenon in itself and in relation to others, *neither desiring nor disliking it*, we will in quiet attentiveness be able to form a clear concept of it, its parts, and its relations. The more we expand our considerations and the more we relate phenomena to one another, the more we exercise the gift of observation that lies within us. If we know how to relate this knowledge to ourselves in our actions, we earn the right to be called intelligent" (my italics).[14]

The right to be called intelligent is not easily won, nor should it be. It is, however, the only worthwhile goal in a society that has been transformed, by the psychotic pursuit of wealth, into a mechanistic nightmare.

In the end, I had to write this book in order to find out why I wanted to write this book. Then, of course, I had to throw it all away and start again. No doubt the old satyr, the "sex maverick," in one of his several guises will appear in these pages. Certainly, the unhappy son, and the man almost crippled with shame and grief for his father's lifelong humiliation will take a bow. The pathetic yet strangely dignified old man who wrote extraordinary love letters to women a third his age, in some cases, letters that weren't even read—well, he cannot be avoided, no matter how unrepresentative he seems. However, if I can catch a glimpse of the merest shadow of the man who transformed himself, alchemically, into a true *voyant*, cleansed of the worst of his conditioning and allied to the natural principles we find best expressed in Daoist-anarchist thought, I will be contented. But the most interesting aspect of Miller, for me, is that he allows us to pose an old question—Are people innately destructive of what is good, or is their destructive behavior the fault of a "system"?—in a new light. He also reminds us that Rimbaud's great experiment—*dérèglement de tous les sens*—is only the first part of a process—that, after the *dérèglement* has allowed us to strip away at least some of the conditioning that our sometimes kindly elders imposed upon us as we grew, thinking it would be better for us, or just plain easier to bear, if we learned how to conform, there is a farther shore of possibility, a shore that we may only find by running away for a time (literally, or figuratively, on roller skates, drugs, or a thirty-two-foot ketch) in order to set our inner sense of order in accord with the natural order, the way the old explorers would synchronize their chronometers with Greenwich Mean Time.

Today the system has finally become unplayable—and Miller was one of the first to see that. Too much is at stake now: the natural world, the purity of our water, the other animals, our own souls. Nobody saw more clearly than Miller did, in his day, that the great tragedy of the industrial age was that, while the workers might have been pitted against the bosses, Communists against Blackshirts, socialists against neoliberals, both sides were committed to that very industrial system—their argument being about terms and conditions—that was degrading their habitat and their minds Only a few sought to dismantle it altogether. Miller also understood that the system was not run by some Great Dictator; it was a vast, labyrinthine communal edifice composed of millions of individual "adjustments." As Hart Crane observed,

> We make our meek adjustments,
> Contented with such random consolations
> As the wind deposits
> In slithered and too ample pockets.[15]

Finally, as a true anarchist, Miller saw that we do not need a glorious leader, or leaders, to save us from the nightmare. What we need, each of us, is to become our own anarchists—which is to say, to unlearn our conditioning and refuse to be led, thus transforming ourselves into free-thinking, self-governing spirits and, if we are fortunate indeed, to become one with the Way.

ON HENRY MILLER

In Praise of Flight

There is no salvation in becoming adapted to a world which is crazy.

—Henry Miller, *The Colossus of Maroussi*

La fuite reste souvent, loin des côtes, la seule façon de sauver le bateau et son équipage. Elle permet aussi de découvrir des rivages inconnus qui surgiront à l'horizon des calmes retrouvés. Rivages inconnus qu'ignoreront toujours ceux qui ont la chance apparente de pouvoir suivre la route des cargos et des tankers, la route sans imprévu imposée par les compagnies de transport maritime. Vous connaissez sans doute un voilier nommé "Désir."

—Henri Laborit, *Éloge de la fuite*

A man wakes. He knows exactly what is going to happen today, or at least he thinks he does (like everyone, he knows that the unexpected might occur at any time, that he might go to see his doctor and be told he has an inoperable cancer, or his girlfriend, who stood by him all through that messy divorce, will call him at the office mid-morning to say that she has met someone else, but he keeps the thought of random harm at bay as well as he is able, usually by means of a combination of superstition, moral duplicity, and steady, if uninventive, self-medication). He knows what will happen today, not necessarily in the details, but in the overall pattern: he will go to work and try to achieve something that matters to him, but he will be subjected to a constant stream of tedious interruptions and dubious bureaucracy. When the phone rings, it will be somebody he doesn't want to talk to; when an e-mail arrives, it will convey yet another pointless demand on his time and energy. He will, in short, spend far too much, and oftentimes all, of his day rendering unto Caesar, and almost none of it doing what he wants to do. What this man needs is not a change in his lifestyle, or a new job, or a new wife. What he needs is *la fuite*.

La fuite: I use the French term (after French surgeon and philosopher, Henri Laborit) because there is no right term in English: "flight" is not only not good enough, but also carries undertones of "running away" to no other end than (cowardly) escape. *La fuite*, as described by Laborit in his extraordinary *Éloge de la fuite* is different.[1] It is a leap of the imagination, a total renewal, a commitment to the soul's logic and, if necessary, a time-out from Caesar's world for long enough that our hypothetical office worker can tear himself open and try to heal what is buried in his frontal cortex, or his heart, or his gut. It is not a simple matter, like *reculer pour mieux sauter*—for that is still to abide by a *societal* logic. It is an act, not of cowardice, but of courage. Gide says it most succinctly: "On ne découvre pas de terre nouvelle sans consentir à perdre de vue, d'abord et longtemps, tout rivage" (One cannot discover new lands unless one consents, for a long time, to lose sight of the shore).[2]

That said, there is nothing grand, or grandiose, about *la fuite*. Conducted in the right spirit, it can have the feel of a game (though it is one of our more common mistakes that, because it is not solemn, we assume that play is also not serious). Play is not only *serious*, it is essential. How, and if, we play is, in fact, a matter of (meaningful) life or death. Here is Miller, in a newspaper interview from the 1970s: "One of my ex-wives, when she left me, walked off with all the furniture—everything a bourgeois home should have she took. I began to get boxes from the grocery store to sit and eat on. I made a little table out of the boxes. I was at home with them and then I got the idea, 'Henry, goddamn it, why don't you buy a pair of roller skates and go roller-skating through the rooms here.' I had a marvellous time."[3] From this example, it is clear that, from the first, *la fuite* defies conventional rationality. We do not embark upon *la fuite* to think about our possible options: on the contrary, we do so when we understand that our *possible* options can only return us to the condition we were in before—which is to say, *governed* by forces outside our own will. *La fuite* is a scrubbing of possible options, a rejection of the societal solution—though only because it seeks to go beyond the usual options, and push back the limits of reasoning. In fact, it's not simply that you *cannot* find a new land until you have courage to lose sight of the familiar shore, the sailor *must* lose sight of that shore—of the old system, the old way of life, the former wife, the possessions and even, in one of Miller's favorite exercises in *la fuite*, that most precious of entities, his homeland.

It should be remembered, though, that *la fuite* only works if the sailor can take it as a given, before weighing anchor, that *everything is permitted to the imagination*. As Miller says, "Imagination is the voice of daring. If there is anything godlike about God, it is that. He dared to imagine everything."[4] Logic has its limits, but there are no actual limits to what could be imagined in a free world. As Terence says, "Homo sum, humani nihil a me alienum puto" (I am human, and nothing human is alien to me).[5] Unless this is the case, *la fuite* is nothing more than a daydream. However, we live in a society bent on limiting, and even denigrating, the imagination (entrepreneurs excepted), and, as any anarchist can tell you, the first obstacle to a just community, in which men and women might govern themselves, is the early and ruthless application of social conditioning to the defenseless child's imagination, a process that begins as soon as he or she is old enough to mimic, to recognize punishment, and to listen. Societal conditioning aims at controlling every aspect of a person's life: body image, sexuality, expectations, sense of home, ability to grieve, earning capacity, societal role and status. Most of all, it seeks to control, to inhibit, and, wherever possible, to stultify the imagination and keep the machinery of Capital supplied with more or less docile operators. That the wastage rate is high is neither here nor there to the "1 percent."

THEORY OF *LA FUITE*

There is much more to *Éloge de la fuite* than can be discussed in the space available here. It is unfortunate, to say the least, that, to date, only two of Henri Laborit's books have been published in English translation.[6] Certainly, Laborit is a fascinating figure, a genuine Renaissance man—scientist in several fields, philosopher, social observer, and maverick—yet he has long been unjustly overlooked and was even denied a Nobel Prize, for purely political reasons.

Henri Marie Laborit was born in Hanoi in 1914. Though he suffered from tuberculosis as a child, he excelled in school and, having gained his *baccalauréat* in Paris, he entered the School of Naval Medicine at Bordeaux (his father, who died of tetanus when Laborit was six years old, had also been a military physician). As a navy surgeon, Laborit began his first researches in anesthesiology, which in turn led to work in pharmaceutical research and, eventually, to the development of chlorpromazine, initially used to treat soldiers suffering from shell shock after World War II, and then later on a wider spectrum of conditions. In spite of the broad range of his research, his work in this area is considered Laborit's principal achievement. Chlorpromazine— also colloquially known as "Laborit's drug"—was marketed as Largactil at the end of 1952, and, though its use as an antipsychotic has been more or less discontinued over the past decade or so, it has been widely used to treat a variety of disorders since that date.[7]

Yet Laborit's contribution to pharmacology is only one aspect of his wide range of interests and achievements, which included biology, town planning, human and animal behavior, biopsychosociology and psychosomatics, as well as social and political science. Nominated for the Nobel Prize in the 1990s, he was passed over for political reasons—for, like Miller, Laborit wasn't just a restless, multi-talented individual; he was also highly independent, a free-thinker who did not follow the party line and did not suffer fools gladly. Most important, he was not to be governed. Indeed, he remained independent throughout his life, receiving no salary (other than his navy pay) or state money to run his laboratories, funding them instead through the sale of patents for his several innovations in pharmaceuticals.

To travel any further on this path would be to digress. My present interest in Laborit is in his theory of *la fuite*, or to paraphrase, his tenet that, at times, *escape is the only way to stay alive and keep dreaming.* However, as he also notes, there are different kinds of escape, and the reasons why we fail to get clear of danger are not always clear. On the first point, it is important that the escapee is driven by a strong desire to change his life, a desire that is usually predicated on refusal of unacceptable, unjust, or stifling environmental conditions, and/or a desire to fulfill a potential that has been denied: "When it can no longer battle the wind and the rough sea, there are two ways a sailboat can continue on its way: by drifting at the mercy of the wind and the tides, or flight before the storm, with a minimum of sail. Often, far from shore, flight becomes the only way to save the ship and its crew. It also allows for the discovery of unknown shores that appear on the horizon after the storm has passed. Unknown shores that lie far from the sea lanes of the great cargo boats and tankers, sea lanes imposed by the great shipping companies. No doubt you have heard of a sailboat called 'Desire.'"[8]

La fuite, then, is a strategy for preserving the integrity of "Désir" in a hostile world that would bend or break that desire to its will—and Laborit is an adept at describing exactly what constitutes "times like these." In his beautifully eloquent, yet profoundly unsettling, conclusion to the book, he provides a catalogue of modern ills (many of them overlap entirely with the diagnoses made by Miller in his social criticism) that appear both overwhelming in their variety and severity, and inexcusable in their blatant injustice. Reading this list, we are obliged to confront an industrialized culture that can no longer be tolerated, yet we seem not to know how to change it. Why? Laborit's suggestion, in part, is that our social conditioning marries each human organism's primal instinct for self-preservation with what societal institutions claim is the greater good of the whole, even though it is blatantly only the good of a privileged few (or, according to another, more generous argument, which sees the compulsion to accrue excess wealth as a kind of psychiatric disorder, the good of nobody at all).

This view depends on a certain understanding of how evolutionary imperatives govern all living organisms and of how social institutions mobilize these imperatives in pursuit of their own organizational ends. According to Laborit, there are four types of behavior in humans: (1) At the most basic level, we *consume*, that is, we satisfy our "basic needs," such as eating, drinking, sleeping, and so forth.[9] As long as these needs are met, we (2) *seek gratification*, that is, whenever we experience a stimulus that causes pleasure, we attempt to repeat it. We can see these behaviors as pre-social in a sense: they will happen in any living organism, as long as the wherewithal for consumption and gratification are at hand. However, the next behavior, (3) a variation on the standard fight-or-flee mechanism, is, in most humans, almost entirely social, or at least, is usually a response to pressure from a social group (family, peers, chain of command, neighbors, community, spouse, among others). This behavior is reactive, an attempt to avoid punishment or aggression, whether by fighting, in hopes of destroying the aggressors, or fleeing (at least temporarily) to avoid them. Finally, there is (4) *inhibition*, when the defeated subject waits anxiously—but passively—for the next uncontrollable, seemingly random occurrence that will "happen to" him. As Laborit notes, anxiety of this kind marks the impossibility of mastering a situation, and it would seem essential, to safeguard the integrity of the individual, to avoid this final behavior at any cost:

Tant que mes jambes me permettent de fuir, tant que mes bras me permettent de combattre, tant que l'expérience que j'ai du monde me permet de savoir ce que je peux craindre ou désirer, nulle crainte: je puis agir. Mais lorsque le monde des hommes me contraint à observer ses lois, lorsque mon désir brise son front contre le monde des interdits, lorsque mes mains et mes jambes se trouvent emprisonnées dans les fers implacables des préjugés et des cultures, alors je frissonne, je gémis et je pleure. Espace, je t'ai perdu et je rentre en moi-même. Je m'enferme au faite de mon clocher où, la tête dans les nuages, je fabrique l'art, la science et la folie.

(As long as my legs allow me to flee, as long as my arms allow me to fight, as long as my experience of the world allows me to decide what I can fear or desire, there is no problem: I can act. But when the human world compels me to observe its laws, when my desire butts its head against the forbidden, when my hands and my legs are imprisoned in the relentless irons of prejudices and cultures, then I shudder, I moan and I weep. Space: I have lost you and I return to myself. I close myself up in my steeple [*clocher*] where, head in the clouds, I manufacture art, science and madness.)[10]

This latter point may seem a little worrying in its apparent agreement with Freud's rather strict notions of how sublimation works. However, it is not suggested as a model to be followed. Beyond that withdrawal into my own space (*clocher*), is the most mature choice of all: *to act* (which, paradoxically, may be the choice to refrain from acting, or rather, the refusal to act as expected). In the end, *la fuite* offers a temporary withdrawal that is not, on the one hand, an ivory tower or false community in which a cruel, ugly world is rejected for the sake of the finer things in life (*clocher* not only means bell tower, or belfry; it can also suggest a narrow parochialism), nor, on the other, a simple breathing space from which to take stock of "real-world" (i.e., societal) options, but a voyage into unknown waters in pursuit of a new way of being.

This form of flight, this game, is possibly Henry Miller's favorite pursuit: he played *la fuite* often, in his personal life, and in his fiction, sometimes by choice, sometimes by contriving social conditions where he had no other option than to strip everything away and begin again. "I have no money, no resources, no hopes. I am the happiest man alive," he says, as *Tropic of Cancer* opens. Later, he notes: "Nobody, so far as I can see, is making use of those elements in the air which give direction and motivation to our lives. Only the killers seem to be extracting from life some satisfactory measure of what they are putting into it. The age demands violence, but we are getting only abortive explosions. Revolutions are nipped in the bud or else succeed too quickly. Passion is quickly exhausted. Men fall back on ideas, *comme d'habitude*."[11]

The beauty of *la fuite* is in going beyond the point where it is possible to fall back on ideas. The era of *comme d'habitude* is over: *now is the time of the assassins*. This idea sits at the center of Miller's world, but, his own life and work notwithstanding, the most elegant, the cruelest, and the most extravagant instance of *la fuite* that he would encounter came from an obscure autobiographical work by a onetime author and sailor from Germany, a man who abandoned everything—family, homeland, passport, identity—to be "one with the sea."

HEIMAT

In 1946, Miller published a substantial review of George Dibbern's *Quest*, the true story of one man's journey from Nazi Germany to New Zealand, where, in his youth, he had spent some time living with the Maori at Dannevirke, after jumping a merchant vessel in Sydney in 1909. Then, in 1918, he was placed in an internment camp for a year before being deported back to Germany. Dibbern seems to have formed strong ties in New Zealand, especially with a Maori woman named Rangi, whom he considered his "spiritual mother." However, he made a genuine effort to settle in Germany, marrying a woman named Elisabeth Vollbrandt in 1921, and setting up as a small farmer in Schleswig-Holstein, where he and Elisabeth had three daughters over the next five years. His attempts at farming were not particularly successful, however, and after several other business ventures failed, he moved to Berlin, where he began to publish short stories based on his experiences among the Maori. Finally, as the situation in Germany became more and more uncertain, he decided to return to his first love—the sea. He had, by now, few assets, but he still had a boat that his brother-in-law had built for him, and, in 1932, he left his family behind and crossed the Atlantic in that newly refurbished vessel, a thirty-two-foot ketch he called *Te Rapunga* (Maori for "Black Sun"), eventually landing in San Francisco after 101 days without touching land. From there, he proceeded via Hawaii to New Zealand, where he found that Mother Rangi had died in his absence. Meanwhile, after death threats were issued from Nazi groups in New Zealand and at home in Germany, Elisabeth refused to make the journey to join her husband, and he was now alone.

At this point, Dibbern made a decisive break with his former life. Because he objected to its Nazi insignia, he refused to sail the German colors on *Te Rapunga* and set about creating a flag of his own (a flag that announced his true *Heimat*, or homeland, as the entire world, not some Aryan nation but the community of life on earth). He also got rid of his passport, replacing it with a document of his own devising. It read: "I, George Dibbern, through long years in different countries and sincere friendship with many people in many lands feel my place to be outside of nationality, a citizen of the world and a friend of all peoples. I recognize the divine origin of all nations and therefore their value in being as they are, respect their laws, and feel my existence solely as a bridge of good fellowship between them. This is why, on my own ship I fly my own flag, why I have my own passport and so place myself without other protection under the goodwill of the world."[12]

This was a bold and dangerous step. Now, like the liegeless knight in an old saga, Dibbern was beyond the pale, traveling under no recognized flag so that, as a citizen of the world, he was nobody's responsibility. Over the next several years, he sailed up and down the American coast, and all around the Pacific, writing his book and spreading his message of international goodwill and kinship until, on February 12, 1941, a month before *Quest* was to be published in New York, *Te Rapunga* was seized and he was once again interned on Somes Island, in Wellington Harbor. Sadly, while it worked against him in all kinds of ways (for example, when he wanted to make a land purchase in the Gulf Islands), being "a man without a country" did not help him avoid internment.

While on Somes Island, Dibbern saw his book published and, after some years, was able to read Miller's extraordinary review (it had finally been published in *Circle* magazine in 1946). Before that, however, he had already received a letter from Miller, in which his new and most ardent admirer wrote:

Your book is a wonderful human document, a spiritual more than a physical saga. I felt that you were a brother, and it's as a brother that I write you and pray that you are well. All your reflections about life, about war, about people, about the Bible, impressed me deeply. So few men think for themselves. That's what made your book a feast. . . . I always wondered, of course, whether you would continue cruising about, whether you would find nothing but disillusionment whenever you put ashore. The purpose of self-liberation, which you seem to have achieved, is to rejoin society but how difficult, especially when it's the kind of world we now have.[13]

As Dibbern was still interned on Somes Island, he may have entertained a slightly different perspective on the question of rejoining society, and we can only guess what he thought when he read these words: "The more you succeed in freeing yourself from passions and prejudices, from stupid fetishes and inhibitions, the less place there is for you in the world. That's how it seems. I know something of what it's all about, because I made a similar struggle all my life. The feeling of being cut off is an agony." As always, it is Miller who occupies center stage—and seems to suffer most—no matter what the drama. Nevertheless, his message, and the passion of his review, led to a lifelong friendship of sorts, during which the two men exchanged many letters, and Miller (always generous when he actually had money) made valiant efforts to help Dibbern's family in Germany after the war. Meanwhile, having married and started a second family in New Zealand, Dibbern's ever-changing luck turned again, when he won £10,000 in the lottery and, even after he generously donated half of the money to a workmate, was able to buy two islands in Tasmania, where he and his second wife, Eileen, set up yet another farm. However, he could not resist going back to sea and did so often, mostly to take part in long-distance races. Inevitably, he and Eileen parted, and, in 1960, he was talking about going back to Germany, in order, he said, to "close the circle." Before he could make that final journey, however, Dibbern died of a heart attack in Auckland, in 1962. His beloved *Te Rapunga* was left in some disrepair for many months after his death, changing hands several times before a man named Ken Moss found the boat "in sad condition sitting under some trees at Bayswater Wharf when he bought her for NZ$800 in 1971."[14]

There's an interesting passage in *Quest*, when George Dibbern tells Elisabeth that he has decided to leave Germany. She is, naturally, unhappy about this sudden development and tries to reason with him, suggesting he try a new line of work and also that he could do more to fit in with society: "When you are in Rome," she says, "you must do as a Roman does." To which Dibbern replies:

If these are the conditions of Rome, who the hell wants to live in Rome? What is the good of adapting myself ninety-nine times? The hundredth time, perhaps when I am tired, I am myself, as I really am, and then they rub their eyes, and call me a traitor because I have suddenly changed. Am I not ninety-nine times a hypocrite? Whom they are right to mistrust? Don't I sell my soul ninety-nine times for a lousy piece of bread? And now I am a relief worker, unemployed, without any future—till the very soul is crushed within me, till I become a beast. Just cringing, afraid to lose my last bone. But I am not meant to be this. And I won't be! How break through—because I must!

—and the conversation continues, a painful confrontation between a desperate man and what Elisabeth can only see as the voice of reason:

Who is going to provide for the children?
Whilst I am trying to answer, some deep inner voice says: *man does not live by bread*

alone. I am shocked to hear myself saying it aloud; it sounds so smug, so like a parson. But suddenly I know it to be the truth. Perhaps it is more important that someday I may be an understanding comrade to the children than be a provider now.

A fine saying you are. Christianity starts at home, my wife answers, full of bitterness.

What use is it to keep on arguing? My mind is made up. I am dead. I therefore packed my things. So little sense of possession have I that I have always felt myself a guest in my own home, and, as an old sailor, I have few belongings. Quickly I make three heaps—one to take along, one to leave behind, and the third to throw away.[15]

It is instructive to compare this passage to the famous lines from *Tropic of Cancer*: "I am living at the Villa Borghese. There is not a crumb of dirt anywhere, nor a chair misplaced. We are all alone here and we are dead."[16] It is interesting, that, in the midst of ordinary life, suffering only the most familiar hardships, that these characters should think of themselves as "dead"—and that the thought should, on one level, lead to a kind of liberation. Reading these lines, one is reminded of the words of Tsunetomo Yamamoto, in *Hagakure, or The Book of the Samurai*: "If by setting one's heart right every morning and evening, one is able to live as though his body were already dead, he gains freedom in the Way." And again: "If a warrior is not unattached to life and death, he will be of no use whatsoever. The saying that 'All abilities come from one mind' sounds as though it has to do with sentient matters, but it is in fact a matter of being unattached to life and death. With such non-attachment one can accomplish any feat."[17]

What more likely way to move beyond attachment to life and death than to come to the sudden realization that one is, in a meaningful sense, already dead? Now, there is nothing to lose or gain. Everything—even a family, even children, even one's homeland—can be set aside in order to realize one's true nature. This may seem cruel, of course (especially when we consider the children in this case), but it does not disturb Miller when he comes to write his review. To Miller, as to any other follower of the Daoist-Anarchist path, what matters is to live according to one's inherent nature. To do otherwise is an offense against the Way. In this context, not to be governed is much more than the personal gesture of a rebel spirit, it is an exemplary choice—but that choice must be seen through to its end. There can be no turning back, no skirting of the familiar shore. When this is the case, when *la fuite* is enacted in its most rigorous form—as an *artful* refusal of "the kind of world we now have"—it becomes an implicit demand for a better world, a world of freedom for all. This is what Miller values in *Quest*: this sense that the most drastic measures must be taken if we are to regain our lives: "Break out or die! That is the decision we all have to make some time or other. Man does not live by bread alone. George Dibbern obeys the inner voice, leaves his wife and children whom he loves, and sets sail. It is an act of desperation, but it is an act! and he is not a man who shuns the consequences of his acts."[18]

As we might expect, what Miller stresses is *Quest*'s exemplary quality, its value as an imaginative enactment of *la fuite*.

The importance of this book, which is really the log of an inner voyage, is in the example it sets forth. Relying solely upon himself, his own inner resources, Dibbern discovers the value of dependency. Out in the middle of the ocean, sitting at the tiller in utter silence for long hours, this man thinks everything out for himself. "One needs distance and aloneness," he says. . . . Not trying is equal to not moving, *which is equal to living death.* Death is the penalty of sin; therefore not moving is sin. . . .

The long voyage is *not an escape but a quest*.
The man is seeking for a way to be of service to
the world. (my italics)

Here is the great paradox of anarchist thinking:
what looks like escapism is, in fact, a grail quest.
As Miller stresses, "Dibbern is not a renegade
or an escapist, fatuous terms, when you think of
it, since the real escapist is the man who adapts
himself to a world he does not subscribe to. No,
it is the purity and integrity of men like Dibbern
which makes it difficult for them to fit into our
world."

But then, may we *not* ask about the children?
The three daughters left behind with their mother
in Nazi Germany? It is clear from the book that
Dibbern did expect Elisabeth and the girls to follow him to New Zealand, and he imagines them
in the place where he had been happiest, among
the Maori people, with his spiritual mother,
Rangi. We can also argue that it was Elisabeth,
not Dibbern, who prevented this from happening: menaced by the Gestapo in Germany, and
fearful for the lives of her daughters, she refused
to undertake the journey that would reunite the
family. By the time the war was over, Dibbern
had spent five years in an internment camp, and
neither he nor Elisabeth had the wherewithal to

realize that plan—and it seems clear that she decided to make a life for herself and her children in Germany.

But then, who is to say what would have happened, had Dibbern remained with his family? Already a person of interest to the Nazis, he might well have ended up in a camp, or worse, and his family might have been condemned with him. Besides, many people fled Europe at that time, and many left families behind, hoping they might follow later. Some did, some did not. Dibbern's family survived—and his daughters were able, a few months after their father's death, to meet Henry Miller in Munich. To this meeting he brought a German edition of *Quest*, published under the title, *Unter eigener Flagge*, with Miller's essay as a preface, by Claassen Verlag. Later, recalling that day, Dibbern's eldest daughter, Frauke Dibbern-Ploog, noted that her mother wasn't particularly impressed, but that she herself had read the book "so wie einen guten Roman gelesen" (as a good piece of fiction), adding that, for her, "dafür war Vater zu sehr entfernt, zu überhöht. Mutter meinte immer, er wäre ein Peter Pan gewesen—ewig Kind bleiben, keine Verpflichtungen haben, mit allen Menschen gut Freund sein" (this father was too remote, too excessive. Mother always said, he was a kind of Peter Pan, he wanted to remain a boy forever, with no obligations, everybody's friend). Maybe she was right, but then, who wants to "grow up" and become adapted to a world that is crazy?

Like a Fluid (The False Pornographer)

I've led a good rich sexual life, and I don't see why it should be left out.

—Henry Miller, *Paris Review* interview

Aimer l'autre, cela devrait vouloir dire que l'on admet qu'il puisse penser, sentir, agir de façon non conforme à nos désirs, à notre propre gratification, accepter qu'il vive conformément à son système de gratification personnel et non conformément au nôtre.[1]

—Henri Laborit, *Éloge de la fuite*

The charge that Miller could not write about "sex with love" is one that he didn't even begin to contest. But then, in his experience, sex-with-love had been reduced to something highly problematic—not by any choices he had made, but by the societal conditioning around love and marriage to which we are all more or less subjected. According to the dominant narrative, love and sex do overlap, briefly, during late courtship and the honeymoon period (according to my own, somewhat causal researches, this might be anywhere from three months to five years or so after the wedding) but from that point on, both parties, male and female, are supposed to get on with their societally defined roles. She, as wife (as distinct a role from lover as can be imagined), is designated mother and nest builder; he, as husband-breadwinner, is considered *manly* based on earnings, social status, and maturity, that is, his ability to conform to a system that has almost nothing to offer him except competition with other men and some kind of pastime, sports, say, or nights out with "the boys." (It is revealing that, as André Dubus has pointed out, whenever a man does anything he considers remotely satisfying, he either does it alone or with other men who are invariably referred to as "the boys").[2] In the 1970s, feminism pointed out how diminished women were by this marriage narrative, but, for some reason, most men pretended they were fine with it, presumably for the same reasons that men are more reluctant than women to seek medical advice when they are ill.

Exhibit 1, then: no sex-with-love scenes in Miller's work. But then, I wonder how anyone would go about writing such scenes. The novel, fiction generally, tends to work in and around problem areas of human experience. Any writer proposing a book to her agent or editor along the lines of "two people meet at a picnic, eat some fried wings, agree that they both prefer Cajun to Texas Barbecue sauce, fall in love, and decide to marry" needn't expect a hefty advance. Fiction is about conflict, loss, irresolution, fear, crime and punishment, adultery, war, and other conflicts. In the novel, as in the real, post-honeymoon world, sex with love (or any sex at all) is something of a luxury.

However, that doesn't mean that sex in fiction, while it may be problematical, should demean or degrade women—any more than it should demean or degrade men. I raise this point because, time and time again, whether from an informed feminist standpoint, or from the censorious Right—who would rather we had no sex at all, in books or anywhere else other than the marital bed (for the purpose of procreation only)—criticism of sexual pornography is never matched by similar disapprobation of those products in which a bowdlerized and hopelessly idealized sex-with-love fantasy is transformed into unrealistic and reductive narratives about both men and women (file under rom-com).

When I was a teenager, my mother would have me borrow such books from the library on her behalf (she was a shy woman, socially, and would not go to the library to choose for herself). I could never remember the titles; they were, to me, both venial and hopelessly interchangeable, but I did recall the cover images, and I could tell what kind of book each was from the characters depicted. Books about the nurse who secretly loves the brilliant young surgeon who, after some misunderstandings, comes to love her too and *then they get married*. Or the aristocratic woman, betrothed to a social "equal" (or preferably a superior, like a Duke) who is secretly in love with the taciturn groom from the stables, who is secretly in love with her too (that's why he's taciturn, you see), and they stumble around in a fog for some two hundred pages before everything clears, the Duke is ditched, and our protagonists come together—and *then they get married*. Or a young actress has a crush on the leading man, leading to various mishaps, and then—part of the pleasure, apparently, is that one could see where this was going—*they get married*. And when people get married in books like this, nobody has to say they all lived happily ever after. They are in love, after all. QED. More recently, our real love affairs are with consumer goods (capitalism's ultimate triumph), with men preferring their game consoles and cars to their partners, and women rating their spouses pretty low after cats, chocolates, and certain varieties of sparkling wine. Naturally, the advertising capitalizes on this. New lover or the boxed set of seasons 1–7 of *The Good Wife*? Hell, life's complicated enough as it is, the customer thinks. So if it's all the same, I'd rather just sit down with a box of chocolates and replay that scene in Series 7 where Jason and Alicia kiss in the elevator.

It would be wrong to claim that such fantasy fictions are as obnoxious or as troubling as the worst examples of pornography, in which the degradation of women is played out physically, as such, and not just implied (e.g., as in the rejection of *actual* men in romance books and TV programs). On the other hand, while some aspects of Miller's work are repellent—as in the extended Ida Verlaine passage from *Sexus* cited in *Sexual Politics*—these are often pastiches, possibly parodies, of soft porn standards that would have been available in his boyhood. Certainly, as has been conceded, *Sexual Politics* is fair as an indictment of how a sexist society's attitudes toward women are reflected in one strand of Miller's writing (it does no harm to note, on the other hand, that Kate Millett is highly selective in her analysis, basing her entire argument on one very ugly—and highly derivative—passage). But this is only one strand, a mode of "manly" talk about sex, inherited from turn-of-the-century pornography like *The Pearl*, *A Man with a Maid*, and, most particularly, given his slight personal connection with Miller's father, the work of Frank Harris (of whom more in the discussion of property, below).

What Millett does not take into account is Miller's stated aversion to the commodification of sexuality in general by a property-based society, on the one hand, or his resistance to the puritan strain in America and western Europe that demeans both men and women, on the other (here, if the source of his loathing was his mother, his immediate literary model was D. H. Lawrence, whose work he wrote about at what some would consider enervating length). Nor does she acknowledge Miller's own self-diagnosis of the emotional and spiritual damage that the cult of manliness inflicted on him, or his efforts to outgrow the legacy of a twice-poisoned childhood (first, by having to witness the steady war of attrition waged by his mother against his supposedly "unmanly" father, and second, the cult of impossible manly virtue that reached its zenith as Miller was growing up, with Teddy Roosevelt as its highest model and Frank Harris himself as its sexual master of ceremonies).[3] It also seems important to note that, in spite of his mother's influence, in spite of that manliness cult, and in spite of his farcical relationship with June, Miller evinces more affection for actual (as opposed to idealized or demonized) women than many of his contemporaries. Finally, I might add that, aside from the distastefully triumphalist passage that Millett selects to condemn Miller overall, a great deal of his writing reveals him as powerless, degraded, humiliated,

and rejected in any number of unmanly ways—
and it is here that he is at his most honest, in the
major novels. To damn him to hell on the basis
of a specific, possibly parodic passage in one of
his lesser works seems more than a little unfair,
on a level with judging Nabokov's personal character on the basis of a literal reading of the first
fifty pages or so of *Lolita*.

That Miller is a product of his times is clear.
As I have noted, his writings about sex all too
frequently follow in the soft pornographic tradition of the anonymously authored *Pearl*, or
Man with a Maid books, or the "adventures" of
Frank Harris—a tradition in which manliness
is preserved by the exercise of power (though it
should also be remembered that, when Miller,
perennially short of cash, took to writing "smut"
for money, his output was quite often sent back
as not being smutty enough. It would appear that
these mercenary tales contained more storyline
than the average reader of soft pornography requires). The typical narrative of this tradition
shows the man as masterful, confident, utterly in
control, while the woman is gradually reduced
from an initial position of prudish resistance to
obedient and grateful slave. This transformation
is achieved by a combination of the hero's mastery and the lucky victim's cravings for the plea-
sures that only he can give her:

Soothingly, I passed my right hand over Alice's quivering bottom and stroked it caressingly, alleviating in a wonderfully short time the pain. In spite of the severity of the whipping she had received, she was not marked at all! Her flesh was like that of a baby, slightly pinker perhaps, but clean and fresh. As I tenderly restored her to ease, her tremblings died away, her breath began to come more freely and normally, and soon she was herself again.

"Well, has the nonsense been whipped out of you, Alice?" I asked mockingly. She quivered but did not answer.

"What, not yet?" I exclaimed, pretending to misunderstand her. "Must I give you another turn?" and I raised the whip as if to commence again.

"No, no!" she cried in genuine terror. "I'll be good!"

"Then lie still and behave yourself," I replied, throwing the whip away into a corner of the room.[4]

All of this is highly ritualized and, of course, it is important that the victory over the woman does not require too much force, for that would give the impression that our hero is not as attractive as he pretends. As Millett points out, in her analysis of the seduction of Ida Verlaine in

Sexus: "In accord with one of the myths at the very heart of a Miller novel, the protagonist, who is always some version of Miller himself, is sexually irresistible and potent to an almost mystical degree. It is therefore no very great surprise to the reader that Ida falls into his hands."[5]

We need hardly point out that Henry Miller did not invent the myth of the mystically potent, irresistible protagonist; this manly man is a staple, not only of Victorian pornography, but of popular fiction generally. At the same time, Miller understood that the myth was heightened by showing, as in Frank Harris's coming-of-age narrative *My Life and Loves*, how the manly man learns to understand the "moods" of his chosen prey. Sensitivity is, at times, a virtue: to win over is often more enjoyable than to overwhelm. The following passage, in which our hero wins the love of a girl called Jessie, a fellow passenger on a boat to America, shows Harris enjoying a subtler kind of power, a mix of skilled "lascivious touchings" and self-restraint that further enhances his manly character, even as he defers actual conquest:

> What a gorgeous afternoon we had! I had learned enough now to go slow and obey what seemed to be her moods. Gently, gently I caressed her sex with my finger till it opened

and she leaned against me and kissed me of her own will, while her eyes turned up and her whole being was lost in thrills of ecstasy. When she asked me to stop and take my hand away, I did her bidding at once and was rewarded by being told that I was a "dear boy" and "a sweet" and soon the embracing and caressing began again. She moved now in response to my lascivious touchings and when the ecstasy came on her, she clasped me close and kissed me passionately with hot lips and afterwards in my arms wept a little and then pouted that she was cross with me for being so naughty. But her eyes gave themselves to me even while she tried to scold.[6]

There is power in the giving of pleasure, a power that comes, not just from seeing the other "lost" in her ecstasy, but also from seducing the woman from the moral scruples she has been taught. She tries to scold, but she cannot; she says she is cross at him for being so naughty, but she is as much a participant in that naughtiness as he is. Significantly, all these lascivious touchings are committed under the very nose of Jessie's father, a fierce, overbearing Scottish Chief Engineer, who epitomizes the puritanical, joyless norms of conventional society. This is a victory indeed: not only does Harris show enviable control, both of himself and the situation, as cunning interloper, armed only with his native wit and youthful charm; he also defeats puritanism as a whole, in the form of the Chief Engineer.

It is not until the ship reaches America that, with Jessie as his willing accomplice, the young man finally consummates his lust. He now settles down to enjoy the fruits of a long and careful campaign—but Jessie has her own surprise in store:

> That very afternoon I took Jessie for a walk in the Park, but when we had found a seat in the shade she confessed that her sister thought we ought to be engaged, and as soon as I got steady work we could be married: "A woman wants a home of her own," she said, "and oh, Boy! I'd make it so pretty! And we'd go out to the theatres and have a gay old time."
>
> I was horrified; married at my age, no, Sir! It seemed absurd to me and with Jessie. I saw she was pretty and bright, but she knew nothing, never had read anything: I couldn't marry her.

This is the next lesson our hero has to learn—and it is a painful one. A man may win victory in the short term over an individual woman but, in the long term, he is in greater danger. For, as soon as she sets her sights on marriage, a woman becomes an agent of the puritan enemy, working undercover to lure the man into a life of "steady work" and responsibility. It's the same lesson we learn in every hard-boiled detective or spy movie: the woman can't be trusted, she has her own agenda, and sex is only a staging post on the way to her ultimate goal. We recognize that this agenda is learned—ingrained from birth as part of the socialization process—but it is no less powerful for that. And if the woman wins this battle, the man is done for.[7] There is no greater, or more disgraceful self-betrayal in human affairs than the transformation that changes a *man* into a *husband*. What follows, inevitably, is a kind of self-defeat. If boys do not learn this from observation (of their own fathers, of neighbors and kin), then they must learn it the hard way. And this is why the priapic alter-ego in Miller's work is angry: promised power and independence by the long tradition of manly literature, he finds that every woman he meets (other than some impossible, idealized beauty) is a potential snare.

This perspective on marriage (and "relationships" generally) will be unpopular with (and dismissed by) many readers, but it arises, not from conviction, but from observation. As a teenager in the late 1960s and early '70s, I used to wonder why "The System" got so het up whenever it was faced with the least sign that men and women—or boys and girls, at least—might be able to create new paradigms for sex and love, following the precepts of mutual respect and openness that were being voiced around that time. Ideas like those expressed by Henri Laborit in the epigraph to this chapter seemed at once self-evident (to us) and dangerously idealistic (to the powers-that-be).

Laborit further elaborates on this idea in *Éloge de la fuite*, pointing out that the main obstacle to our accepting the other on this level is a deep-grained social conditioning in which our relationships have been engineered in terms of possession and appropriation—in short, the potential for an intimate, mutually tolerant and mutually curious relationship between equals has been sacrificed to a property-based social paradigm. None of this was ever news. What was surprising, for some of us, was how ferocious the backlash against such analyses was back in the 1960s and '70s, whether it struck back at open relationships, radical feminism, an increased openness among lesbians and gay men, or even those marriagelike relationships into which people were entering without drawing up the prescribed property-based contract. That backlash seemed mysterious to me—to begin with. Now, however, looking back at that era, it becomes clear that the capitalist society I thought we were overthrowing was not only as strong as ever, but that it would not rest until everything—every object, every "resource," every human activity, every need—*everything* became a commodity. This included love, sex, and romance—all of them big earners in an ideal consumer society.

For example: everybody knows how expensive a wedding can be (the range is anywhere between "Are you serious?" and "Pass me the Cozaar, now"). Meanwhile, it costs American couples an average of about $20,000 to get divorced,[8] and, according to figures drawn up by the US government, around 50 percent of marriages end in divorce. To put this in perspective, that means there is one divorce every thirty-six seconds or so,[9] or to put that another way: 2,400 divorces per day, 16,800 divorces per week, and 876,000 divorces a year. The average length of a marriage that ends in divorce is eight years. No need to do the math to see that marriage and divorce provide healthy revenue streams to any number of industries every year. Meanwhile, there are those who believe there is a direct relationship between the inevitable sexual and romantic disappointment inherent in turning our most basic desires and needs (not just for sex, however that happens, but for the real basics of touch and mutuality) into an institution and the huge sums of money spent on the various diversions and consolations on offer in a property-based society. Even if we leave aside the debate over confectionery (with one UK survey, as noted above, suggesting that more than half of all women prefer chocolate to sex) and sentimentality-porn, we might justifiably wonder why, if married love is so satisfying, the value of the more or less mainstream porn industry averages out, when a number of estimates are reconciled, at somewhere near $13 billion in the United States alone. Meanwhile, an Urban Institute study found that, across just eight American cities, the underground sex economy's worth in 2007 was estimated between $39.9 and $290 million.[10] Clearly, the unfulfilling marriage is a money-spinner for all kinds of businesspeople— which suggests that it may well be time to start asking (yet again) what is wrong with the institution of marriage per se. Or maybe we should be asking another question altogether.

As noted above, Henry Miller, like the Wife of Bath, married five times. Late in life, he described four of these as accidents: "I was trapped you might say. I don't know myself how I fell into them," but he made an exception for June Mansfield, who, he says mysteriously, "helped me."[11] It's an odd claim to make—especially considering the lengths to which he went in persuading his third wife, Janina Lepska, to abandon not only her family in New York but also a philosophy scholarship at Yale so she could move, with a much older man, into what wasn't much more than a shack at Big Sur. But then, Miller had a complex view of what marriage involved, or should involve—and it is this, and the echo it allowed him of his parents' dreadful marriage (an echo he sought, perhaps, in order to revise the imbalance of power he had witnessed there) that may have driven him to play the game, on his own estimate, four times too often. Here he is, in a revealing, less obviously parodic passage from *Sexus*, reflecting on power relations between the sexes:

> How we hate to admit that we would like nothing better than to be the slave! Slave and master at the same time! For even in love the slave is always the master in disguise. The man who must conquer the woman, subjugate her, bend her to his will, form her according to his desires—is he not the slave of his slave? How easy it is, in this relationship, for the woman to upset the balance of power! The mere threat of self-dependence, on the woman's part, and the gallant despot is seized with vertigo. But if they are able to throw themselves at one another recklessly, concealing nothing, surrendering all, if they admit to one another their interdependence, do they not enjoy a great

and unsuspected freedom? The man who admits to himself that he is a coward has made a step towards conquering his fear; but the man who frankly admits it to everyone, who asks that you recognize it in him and make allowance for it in dealing with him, is on the way to becoming a hero. Such a man is often surprised, when the crucial test comes, to find that he knows no fear. Having lost the fear of regarding himself as a coward he is one no longer: only the demonstration is needed to prove the metamorphosis. It is the same in love. The man who admits not only to himself but to his fellow men, and even to the woman he adores, that he can be twisted around a woman's finger, that he is helpless where the other sex is concerned, usually discovers that he is the more powerful of the two. Nothing breaks a woman down more quickly than complete surrender. A woman is prepared to resist, to be laid siege to: she has been trained to behave that way. When she meets no resistance she falls headlong into the trap.

And he continues:

To be able to give oneself wholly and completely is the greatest luxury that life affords. Real love only begins at this point of dissolution. The personal life is altogether based on dependence, mutual dependence. Society is the aggregate of persons all interdependent. There is another richer life beyond the pale of society, beyond the personal, but there is no knowing it, no attainment possible, without first traveling the heights and depths of the personal jungle. To become the great lover, the magnetiser and catalyser, the blinding focus and inspiration of the world, one has to first experience the profound wisdom of being an utter fool. The man whose greatness of heart leads him to folly and ruin is to a woman irresistible. To the woman who loves, that is to say. As to those who ask merely to be loved, who seek only their own reflection in the mirror, no love however great, will ever satisfy them. In a world so hungry for love it is no wonder that men and women are blinded by the glamour and glitter of their own reflected egos. No wonder that the revolver shot is the last summons. No wonder that the grinding wheels of the subway express, though they cut the body to pieces, fail to precipitate the elixir of love. In the egocentric prism the helpless victim is walled in by the very light which he refracts. The ego dies in its own glass cage.[12]

Here we see why, for Miller, the man finds himself in such a bind when it comes to

sex-with-love, which he seems to see as predicated upon some kind of slavery. On the one
hand, he desires women for the pleasure they
offer, but he hates them for the twin dangers they
present: the first, as we have noted, is that every
woman is an agent of society, a means by which
that society seeks to control and domesticate
him; second, if his desire (love?) for the woman is
great, or if it becomes too evident, he may be ren-
dered truly helpless. She may choose to withhold
from him the sexual responses he needs to feel
manly and in control and if he cannot *command*
such responses, the Roosevelt Man may come
to despise himself for his unmanliness. Miller
was particularly sensitive to such questions, for,
throughout his early years, he had witnessed the
incessant humiliation imposed upon his father
by a hard, puritanical woman who could never
be satisfied (in material terms), and for a large
part of his life, he wondered if, like his father, he
too was not manly enough. Because she treated
his father, first, and then her children, so badly,
Miller never made any secret of his loathing for
his mother; indeed, he waxed bitterly lyrical on
the subject on many occasions:

> Like Madame Rimbaud, my mother was the
> Northern type, cold, critical, proud, unforgiv-
> ing, puritanical. My father was of the South,

of Bavarian parents, while Rimbaud's father was Burgundian. There was a continual strife and clash between mother and father, with the usual repercussions upon the offspring. The rebellious nature, so difficult to overcome, here finds its matrix . . . the demon of revolt had taken possession of me at a very early age. It was my mother who implanted it in me. It was against her, against all that she represented, that I directed my uncontrollable energy. . . . I felt her shadow across my path constantly. It was a shadow of disapproval, silent and insidious, like a poison slowly injected into my veins.[13]

And again, in a late interview: "When I finally found the courage to write what I'd been storing up for years, it came pouring out into one long relentless tirade. Beginning with the earliest memories of my mother, I had saved up enough hatred, enough anger, to fill a hundred books."[14]

For Miller, his mother was a template for the loveless, judgmental, joyless wife whose entire view of her husband, and of the quality and potential of married life, is based on property. No matter how funny, or tender, or kind he may be, the wife sees a man who does not *provide* as unmanly—and, in his earlier years at least, Miller had a horror of being perceived in that light. But what is manliness? In our time, that sounds like such an old-fashioned question, but for Miller and his peers, it was critical—and it is hard not to believe that, even now, in spite of the old-fashioned nature of the term, the idea of what is manly (and what is not) haunts many of us still. For the most part, however, is has to do, not with sex so much, as with property in all its myriad forms.

On Love and Property

> I made up my mind that I would hold onto noth-
> ing, that I would expect nothing.
>
> —Henry Miller, *Tropic of Cancer*

> Little Matty Groves, he lay down and took a little
>   sleep.
> When he awoke, Lord Darnell he was standing at
>   his feet.
>
> Saying "How do you like my feather bed? And
>   how do you like my sheets?
> How do you like my lady who lies in your arms
>   asleep?"
>
> "Oh, well I like your feather bed, and well I like
>   your sheets.
> But better I like your lady gay who lies in my arms
>   asleep."
>
> —"Matty Groves" (traditional ballad)

1971. Carole King is singing "Will You Still Love Me, Tomorrow?" and my girlfriend and her girlfriends are singing along, wanting to know, *seriously*, if some real or imagined tonight's-the-night date with the boy of their dreams is going to be a lasting treasure, or nothing more than a moment's pleasure—as if these two were mutually exclusive, as if something that drags on (for how long? a month? a year? a lifetime?) is better than the vital moment, as if the safest assumption is that the boy is only "out for what he can get" (which is presumably a one-night-stand of fumbled teenage sex) and isn't interested in anything else, whether it be his own pop-song version of romance or a possible, though at this point speculative, wish to engage in a long-term exploration of a beloved other. The key term stated here, however, is the one that reveals the true nature of the bargains and exchanges men and women have been trained to make since their first school disco, and that is the word "treasure." Sooner or later, it will take all but the most callow (or calculating) sweet-talking guy by surprise, but what he is entering into on the dance floor is an improvised contract, in which the *experience* of sexual love is exchanged for a tacit commitment to a property arrangement. The experience in the moment means little—it's "just" a moment's pleasure. Actually, according to the core program of the puritan society in which these two lovers operate, any kind of pleasure is a "just"—because the lasting treasure is, and always will be, the trump card. This isn't about tonight, or a moment; it's about whether this boy solemnly swears to have and to hold this girl, from this day forward, for better for worse, for richer for poorer, in sickness and in health, to love and to cherish, till death they do part, according to God's holy ordinance *and*, moreover, whether he pledges to worship her with his body (what does that even mean?) and to endow her with all his worldly goods (ah!), in the name of the Father, and of the Son, and of the Holy Ghost. To which the only possible responses are:

a) Are you kidding me?;
b) How come it's just me that gets to do the worshipping and endowing of worldly goods? and/or;
c) On consideration, might I ask why we can't hope that this moment might be part of a rich, continuing narrative that, while it may not last forever, might nevertheless offer vital moments of happiness and pleasure, and even emotional and spiritual growth for both parties, at least for a time, through adaptation to and sometimes awe and wonder at the other's complex and mysterious person? Can you really insist on anything more than that? And—anyhow:

Why does it have to be so "lasting"? If, by chance (or is it "destiny"?), two people meet for one astonishing day, or week, or month but, for circumstances beyond their control, are obliged to move on, is that inferior to other experiences of romantic love? If you read the literature, it would actually seem to be more desirable: a clean narrative, no haggling over the worldly goods, the (possibly lasting) nobility that comes of accepting the inevitable, while whispering, as the plane prepares to take off in the tropic heat: "We'll always have Paris . . ." Besides—

Can the party of the first party not see that, by making sexual pleasure an object of barter (a commodity, in effect), it is s/he (yes, it goes both ways, of course it does) who is cheapening the experience? *Now* the deal is: I give you my heart, so what do I get in return?

Of course, it was worse in Miller's time—and the pornography of that age is rife with crude tales of how this mercantile spirit in the woman (or those who sit darkly behind her, urging caution) is outmaneuvered by the cunning of Frank Harris or one of his many surrogates. That tale, of course, is his to keep forever, a commodity in itself, and it has all kinds of uses in the real business of a man's life, namely, his power relations with other men. Of this more later.

Some boys (though not all) will learn that this girl who is "making love" to them, not for pleasure, but as part of a trade agreement, isn't really the girl they were looking for, even if they weren't exclusively concerned with a quickie in the bushes à la *My Life and Loves*. But what to do? The obvious answer (to a young boy, sometimes the only answer) is to become disillusioned and rebel. This rebellion, at its crudest, could be a simple matter of playing the game according to the societal rules, a game at which nobody is more adept than the lapsed romantic. After all, he once had the emotions he must now feign in order to get what he has come to think is "all" he wants (and that "all" is critical, and deeply dispiriting. That 'all' informs almost all pornography, demanding that the object of desire is, not only once it has been enjoyed, but even from the start, even at the point of arousal, also and equally designated an object of contempt). In short, this is a game in which both players have been accorded the role of cheat from the first. Neither is to blame, however. This is social conditioning, practiced under a finely honed system, on innocent, defenseless children, pretty much from infancy.

Women suffer most under this system, without a doubt. For present purposes, however, I want to ask why it is that so many men who start out as romantics end up so damaged and deformed when they lapse. Is it because, like the lapsed Catholic I once was, they need to mock on a more or less continuous basis the faith they once held so fervently? Is he like an old friend of mine, brought up by strictly orthodox Jews, who spent his later years contriving elaborate lunches of shellfish and ham-and-cheese sandwiches in the hope of breaking every possible rule of Kashrut that he could in one sitting? (Of course, he would then serve these up with matzahs and homemade knishes). In much the same way, the lapsed romantic, if he does not fall into the pornographer's camp, may choose to become that most ambiguous of figures—the unwitting rake (a paper-thin disguise, just another trickster face from the ancient gallery, but surprisingly effective, especially if it comes with a visible mark of injury, such as a scar, or a limp, or a psychic wound of some sort). Needless to say, this mask is at the very least half-animal: fox or wolf being the guise of preference—as in the old ballad, *The Mountains High*:

One evening in my rambles two miles below
    Pimroy,
I met a farmer's daughter all on the mountains
    high,
Her beauty so enticed me, I could not pass
    her by,
So with my gun I'll guard her, all on the
    mountains high.
I said my pretty creature I'm glad to meet
    you here,

On these lonesome mountains, your beauty
	shines so clear,
She said kind sir, be civil, my company
	forsake,
For it is my opinion I fear you are some rake.
Said he I am no rake, I'm brought up in Venus'
	train,
I'm seeking for concealment, all in the judge's
	name,
Oh! if my parents they did know your life
	they would destroy,
For keeping of my company, all on the moun-
	tains high.
I said my pretty creature don't let your parents
	know,
For if you do they'll ruin me and prove my
	overthrow,
This pretty little young thing she stood all in
	amaze,
With eyes as bright as Amber upon me she
	did gaze.
Her ruby lips and cherry cheeks, the lass of
	Firmadie,
She fainted in my arms there, all on the
	mountains high,
When I had kissed her once or twice, she
	came to herself again,
And said kind Sir be civil and tell to me
	your name.

Go down in yonder forest, my castle there
    you'll find,
Well wrote in ancient history, my name is
    Rynadine:
Come all you pretty fair maids, a warning take
    by me,
Be sure you quit night walking, and shun bad
    company,
For if you don't you are sure to rue until the
    day you die
Beware of meeting Rynadine all on the moun-
    tains high.

There is, in these old accounts, something supernatural about the romantic seducer: first, he comes from a world that is not defined in the narrow terms that apply here; second, he belongs to the spirit (Tam Lin) or animal (Rynadine) realm, or, at the very least, to another caste, tribe, or social class. However, in all these cases, what matters most is that the liaison has nothing to do with property. It is of the moment; it will not lead to a contract, and it will probably end in estrangement from present societal values ("Death and the Lady") escape into the wild wood ("The Raggle-Taggle Gypsies"), or bloody murder ("Matty Groves").

One of the most important lessons we learn from the ballads is that men have to be wary of other men. The surface narrative is usually competition over a woman, but scratch the surface and the real drama is the getting, or keeping of *property* (women actually *were* property when the ballads were composed, and they are treated, in many of the narratives, as gifts or tokens of exchange between father and husband). As long as a man's property (which might include his money, his possessions, "his" woman, his standing, his beliefs, his prejudices, and his stories) is not threatened, as long as he has, and feels confident about, what he thinks are his just deserts, all is well. When his property is threatened, however, the human male can become exceedingly dangerous. As John Stoltenberg notes, "The world of other men is a world in which we live behind a barrier—because we need to for safety, because we understand there is something about other men that we know we have to protect ourselves from. The world of other men is also a world in which we know we are sized up by other men and judged by other men and sometimes threatened by other men. The world of other men can be, we know, a scary and dangerous place."[1]

The basis for these judgments by other men is either physical prowess or property. As Miller remarks, wistfully, in *Tropic of Capricorn*, money is the ultimate armor—and yet, at the same time, there is never enough of it, there must always be more: "To walk in money through the night crowd, protected by money, lulled by money, dulled by money, the crowd itself a money, the breath money, no least single object anywhere that is not money, money, money everywhere and still not enough, and then no money or a little money or less money or more money, but money, always money, and if you have money or you don't have money it is the money that counts and money makes money, but what makes money make money?"[2]

So it is that, when men come together, property relations of some kind are never far away. Even in the most (seemingly) congenial circumstances, a drinking party, say, the crucial, if unstated, terms of engagement are what a man has, what a man can buy, what a man can refuse, and, most of all, what a man can say and get away with. In this man's world, my property is my *being*: the more I have, the more I am. It is important, however, to remember that this is not *just* about money or possessions. A man's property includes his physique, personality, character, social skills, dress and grooming (or his deliberate contempt for such things), and, of course, his sexual possessions, whether publicly visible or privately reputed. His beautiful wife. His beautiful mistress. Where, presently, he lacks visible property, what comes into play is the list of assets that he can lay claim to—the most obvious of these being sexual adventures, told with relish and defiance, often to an incredulous audience. Back in the 1960s, at my poor, working-class Catholic school, where nobody had anything much by way of physical property, the first thing any moderately imaginative boy acquired was a narrative in which, absurdly, he enjoyed miraculously smooth and dexterous sex with an older girl (a neighbor, say, or a little number he'd met on holiday, or even a grown woman whose stuck-up husband, it was implied, couldn't satisfy her) and that story, if believed, or even half-believed, became an *asset*, an item of virtual property that this boy owned, even if many of those he regaled with his exploits doubted, at the very least, his competency in the matter (the most obvious question being: where did *he* acquire these skills, when the listener knew himself to be completely inept with a bra strap, a zipper, or even the obligatory "pick-up" line). Naturally, such stories were openly mocked, doubted, and immediately subjected to severe cross-examination, but if that boy had enough barefaced cheek (I choose my words carefully here), then what he said was grudgingly accepted—after all, it *could* have happened—and, if another boy dared to point out how unlikely it all sounded, once the initial trial had been concluded, the entire gang would immediately turn on him and demand to know what *he* had done, if he was such a damned expert.

Clearly, what mattered most here was chutzpah. The test wasn't factual credibility, but credible telling, the degree of confidence required. But what exactly does "chutzpah" mean? Jack Achiezer Guggenheim makes the following argument:

> A federal court in the Northern District of Illinois noted in a decision a couple of years ago that *chutzpah* means shameless audacity; impudence; brass. Leo Rosten's *The Joys of Yiddish* defines *chutzpah* as a Yiddish idiom meaning "gall, brazen nerve, effrontery." But neither English translation can do the word justice; neither definition can fully capture the *audacity simultaneously bordering on insult and humor* [my italics] which the word *chutzpah* connotes. As a federal district court in the District of D.C. noted in 1992 that *chutzpah* is "*presumption-plus-arrogance* [my italics] such as no other word, and no other language can do justice to."[3]

When we consider these remarks carefully in the context of men's sexual stories and banter (and indeed, any run-of-the-mill, "soft" works of pornography like *A Man with a Maid*, or the sexual oeuvre of Frank Harris, or indeed, Henry

Miller's cruder sexual anecdotes, such as the Ida Verlaine episode in *Sexus*), the connections soon become evident. The sexual braggart is, in his own eyes, audacious: he will often have his way with his target in a public place, or right under the nose of her puritan father, fiancé, or husband; his main defense for his actions—or rather, how he shrugs them off—is to insist that, in the end, this has all been just a bit of fun, a delightful romp from which everyone emerges satisfied (as never before, in the case of the breathless, ecstatic target) and even, perhaps, a little more liberated from the stuffy mores of the day. However, while these aspects of the story (the audacity, the humor) are open and public, the third (the implied insult) is tacit, though never wholly concealed. Normally, a man is, or is supposed to be, only as good as his word, and if he tells what is clearly an outright lie, his esteem with the group will fall. But the braggart tells a lie that is *insultingly* audacious, *insultingly* unlikely—and then he waits, expectantly, for his audience to show their admiration, and so their confirmation, of his prowess, through conspiratorial, openly collaborative, and, in situations where the power stakes are high, *congratulatory* laughter. In short, he presumes on his fellows' regard. But then, the point of his story was never its veracity (nor is it contempt for the woman, or not primarily).

These stories have almost nothing to do with women, in fact: they are part of a continuous power game played by men, with other men— *exclusively*—and the point of that game is to demonstrate power via a narrative in which the object in contention is not the woman's honor, or her body, but an audacious, insulting, *in your face* appropriation of narrative itself. *Now* the story becomes true because if I say it happened, *then it happened*, no matter how incredible the factual narrative appears to be. This is what makes it an item of property; this is what makes it mine, and not yours. Traditionally, "dirty stories" and "sex jokes" have been seen as vehicles for male solidarity, in that they are, mostly, told against women—and there is no doubt whatsoever that this is often the case. However, observed in another light, we can see that they underpin solidarity among certain males within a group and, in such cases, they are told, in exclusively male society, to cow, instruct, and contain other men.

Without a doubt, this was the world in which Henry Miller grew up. He would sit in his father's tailor shop, when Frank Harris or one of his ilk came by for a fitting, and listen to the great lover regale whoever might be present with his tales—and not only did the young Henry absorb these stories, he also stole and reshaped them to his own ends in later life. He knew what his father's home life was like; Harris probably knew it too. No doubt both, in their very different ways, could picture old Heinrich whispering drunkenly to some private image of a wife who no longer existed, asking her what she wanted from him, wondering how he could win back, if not her love, then at least her respect. How could she have forgotten the boy in him, how can she be so blind to the linger of something wild behind his tongue, a wildness to which, he likes to believe, she once answered back in kind? He thought she had accepted a husband, when all she really wanted was a breadwinner. It must have hurt, to witness such scenes: Heinrich a little tipsy and laughing politely—laughing as the rake triumphs over the unmanly man who cannot win, or satisfy (or, failing that, command) the fair maid, all the time at least half-aware that he is being obliged to laugh at himself.

No wonder, then, that when we read a passage like the bathroom scene in *Sexus* we are, or should be, aware that we are being treated to a stock scenario straight out of the *Pearl / Man with a Maid / My Life and Loves* tradition of the previous generation, something so obviously formulaic that it's hard to imagine anyone taking it as anything other than pastiche. In much—though, crucially, not all—of Miller's writings about sex, Frank Harris lives on, for reasons that are more complicated than they first seem. However, the subjugation of Ida only shows us one aspect of Miller's sexual philosophy. (He hates women, especially women who undermine their husbands, as his target here clearly does, because they remind him of his mother, and how she constantly undermined her husband. Add to this the insult that Harris frequently ordered and took delivery of suits from Miller *père* without paying for them, knowing the little tailor would not object, and might even consider it a privilege, and the picture is complete.) Fucking Ida every which way in her own bathroom, while also living off her husband, makes Val (Miller's alter ego for *Sexus*) a master of chutzpah. Through Val, Miller not only becomes everything his father was not—effortlessly in control, defender of his sex, a man who takes his pleasure where he finds it—he also uses his power over Ida—who, as Millett points out, "like a bullied child, is continually taking orders for an activity which in the hero's view degrades her while it aggrandizes him"—to turn the tables on a joyless, nagging mother figure. Yet the real offense of the Ida passage is that this is not a story to be shared, as part of a communal narrative. Instead, like the works of Frank Harris and the various Anons who give us our pornography, it is a story that appropriates, a story based upon presumption-plus-arrogance, in which the protagonist not only puts one over on his victim, but also on his listeners.

In most of his enterprises, my own father failed so thoroughly and consistently as to inspire a certain warped admiration in his children and some of his neighbors, if not his wife. Most thorough and consistent of all was his failure to regulate his drinking; no one I have ever known took the pledge more frequently or lost his resolve more quickly: at most, a few days of hopeful penitence would pass before he found the next temptation impossible to resist and staggered home with empty pockets or brand new bruises around his eyes and mouth. And yet, though nobody else ever believed it when he declared that this time, *this* time, he really had control of things, I believe that he did, quite sincerely, have days when he was sure he had cracked the complex inner code that drove him onward in his revels, after the rest of the company had decided that it was time to go home. Even in his later years, when he knew what he was doing to his body, he could not desist—and he died, as everyone had more or less predicted, on the floor of the club he most often frequented, in the industrial New Town that had lured him south from West Fife to the English Midlands, then made him redundant at a time when there was no hope of finding any other gainful employment or of "going home." All his life he had been a liar, sometimes a gifted one: at his funeral, I met men who believed, without a doubt, that he had once played professional football, that he had traveled around the world (he had been to Palestine while serving in the RAF), and that he had been raised by a polymath who had given up the chance of fame and fortune to serve his church (in fact, my father was a foundling, who never knew his parents and was passed from family to well-meaning but impoverished family all the while he was growing up). "The heart lies of itself because it must," says a character in Jack Gilbert's poem "Naked but for the Jewelry."[4] My father lied because his life would have been barren without those stories, but also because, no matter what else he might lack, he had the chutzpah to make those stories credible. In fact, that was all he had. Interestingly, however, he never talked about sex, and though it was clear that his marriage was far from satisfactory, he insisted, till the day he died, that my mother was the only woman he had ever loved.

But then, my father's notions of manliness were mostly to do with physical prowess and the ability to endure hardship—work, pain, mental fight—without complaint. Though he was somewhat younger than Henry Miller, he would probably have been exposed to similar idealizations of manly life, of the kind to which Theodore Roosevelt subscribed: "We need the iron qualities that go with true manhood. We need the positive virtues of resolution, of courage, of indomitable will, of power to do without shirking the rough work that must always be done."[5] What the industrial society wanted from my father was physical endurance in the coal mine or the steel mill, and reasonable courage in warfare. It had no use for his narrative gifts. Like Miller, my father saw through the societal rhetoric, but he did not know how to avoid his fate as a piece of industrial cannon fodder.

Yet there is another model of manhood that differs, both from Roosevelt's iron man and Frank Harris's self-regarding braggart in equal measure. It is a model of the masculine that finds, not its opposite, but its complement, in a related model of the feminine. It is anarchist in its roots and communal in its values, and it goes by many names, but I prefer to use the term "adept"—a term drawn from magic and alchemy that is best defined as "one who owns nothing, but has the use of everything." This figure, part-trickster, part-secular saint, appears in many folk narratives, fairy tales, and songs, either in fully developed form, or in prototype, as in the old ballad "Matty Groves," which begins with the words: "A holiday, a holiday, and the first one of the year" setting, not just the scene, but the psychological dynamic of the piece. It is a holiday, and Matty Groves, Lady Darnell, and the rest of the community are at church, but Lord Darnell is out in the fields "bringing the yearlings home"—that is, attending to property matters (and, in the pagan world where this ballad would have originated, a lord absenting himself from the community on a holiday would have had more significance than a post-Christian reading might suggest). In his absence (and here the ballad reverses the typical Frank Harris seduction story) Lady Darnell invites Matty into her bed, leading to a happy and pleasurable sexual encounter. There is just one problem:

> a servant who was standing by and
>   hearing what was said,
> He swore Lord Darnell he would know before
>   the sun would set.
> And in his hurry to carry the news, he bent
>   his breast and ran,
> And when he came to the broad mill stream,
>   he took off his shoes and swam.

No doubt this man's loyalty to his lord will be materially rewarded later. What is strange is that, as arduous as the servant's journey was, Lord Darnell is home in remarkably short order—still in time, in fact, to catch Matty and his wife *in flagrante*. The lady is asleep, so Lord Darnell interrogates Matty, and we notice that everything he says is expressed in terms of property:

> Little Matty Groves, he lay down and took a
>   little sleep.
> When he awoke, Lord Darnell he was stand-
>   ing at his feet.
>
> Saying "How do you like my feather bed? And
>   how do you like my sheets?
> How do you like my lady who lies in your
>   arms asleep?"

And Matty answers honestly, if somewhat rashly:

> "Oh, well I like your feather bed, and well I
>   like your sheets.
> But better I like your lady gay who lies in my
>   arms asleep"

which leads to the following exchange:

> "Well, get up, get up," Lord Darnell cried, "get
>   up as quick as you can!
> It'll never be said in fair England that I slew a
>   naked man."
>
> "Oh, I can't get up, I won't get up, I can't get up
>   for my life.
> For you have two long beaten swords and I
>   not a pocket-knife."

"Well it's true I have two beaten swords, and
    they cost me deep in the purse.
But you will have the better of them and I will
    have the worse."

We notice again, here, that Lord Darnell sees
the world, first, in terms of property values—his
two beaten swords cost him "deep in the purse" and
second, in terms of social standing: he will not slay
a naked (i.e., unarmed) man, for reputation's sake,
and he will even give Matty the "better" sword, but
he is still guaranteed victory in a fight of this kind,
for a commoner like Matty will not have received
the requisite training in swordsmanship. So, on the
surface, Lord Darnell behaves as a nobleman, but
everything is in his favor, and he knows it. We also
notice that Matty really is "naked": he is himself,
stripped to his essence, with no covering, nothing
to dissemble behind. Soon enough, he is dead and,
roused by the duel, Lady Darnell wakes:

And then Lord Darnell he took his wife and
    he sat her on his knee,
Saying, "Who do you like the best of us, Matty
    Groves or me?"

And then up spoke his own dear wife, never
    heard to speak so free.
"I'd rather a kiss from dead Matty's lips than
    you and your finery."

Lady Darnell immediately rejects everything about the lord, including, and especially, the "finery" that he so values; with him she has never known love, or even the *jouissance* of the few hours she has just spent with Matty—a few hours in which the two, man and woman, lady and commoner, lived and acted as equals. Even dead, she says defiantly, Matty is still preferable to her cold, loveless husband. Darnell's response is, of course, dramatic, but we can't help feeling that it is her rejection of his social position, rather than of himself as such, that angers him:

> Lord Darnell he jumped up and loudly he did bawl,
> He struck his wife right through the heart and pinned her against the wall.

> "A grave, a grave!" Lord Darnell cried, "to put these lovers in.
> But bury my lady at the top for she was of noble kin."

To the end, he still doesn't get what has happened here, his only concern being for social status, as he insists that the burial—to conceal the murder—should reflect *his* lady's "noble" connections.

It has been argued that contemporaries, hearing this story, would have seen Lord Darnell's actions as justified: in a hierarchical, property- and status-based society, adultery, even when the "cheated" spouse is a brute and deserves what's coming, is still a sin (i.e., an offense against the status quo). Yet I do not think this is a very imaginative reading. What is happening here is the emergence of a proto-adept, brought to imaginative awareness of his potential by a woman whose strength and independence are exemplary in a deeply misogynistic society. If only for a moment, Matty has all the good in life that Darnell will never have: free of property concerns, he enjoys the lord's feather bed, his sheets, and, of course, the "Lady gay"—all for their own sake, and not because of their property or status value. But Lord Darnell knows nothing of this. Even after he has killed his wife, his only concern is protocol.

It could also be argued that Lady Darnell and Matty enjoy their loving dalliance only for a short time—but this is the ballad world and, like that of the fairy tale, or Dreamtime stories, the ballad is not concerned with linear time. The *jouissance* of a moment wholly outweighs the calendar and the clock. For Lord Darnell, justice has been served in the world of duration, but he will never know real love, or real enjoyment. His wife, on the other hand, forever knows both and even if this is not *Tristan and Isolde*, her love and her sense of joyful play transcend the death that occurs in "real time." Her last words, "I'd rather a kiss," are a triumphant and scornful negation of the property-based society that chained her to this petty tyrant.

For adherents to such a society, this may be a cautionary tale, a morality story even, but it could just as easily be argued that this is a kind of anarchist fable—and this interpretation of the ballad is what I find most interesting of all: for while some may insist that Lord Darnell has restored *human* order by killing these adulterers, an anarchist would suggest that Matty and the lady are reinstating the natural order, at least for a moment. These lovers may be destroyed by the property ethic (though only in clock time), but their actions fall just one step shy of the anarchist ideal: the way of the adept. In its fullest form, the figure of the adept is one who transcends the property-based society day to day, and to do this, his or her guiding principle—to own nothing, yet have the use of everything—must be based on an informed and continuing understanding of what is needful, both to oneself, and to others. Of course, *Désir* (that ever curious *voilier*) has a role to play, even here, but it is *Désir* accompanied by wisdom, discipline, and a deep sense of the communal. In short, the full adept is the very model of that most misunderstood of figures, the philosophical, earth-loving, pagan anarchist. Of course, for the adept, there will be no narratives of appropriation, no bragging, no insulting displays of chutzpah. How could there be, when there is nothing left to steal?

Henry Miller as Anarchist

Let us do our best, even if it gets us nowhere.
 —Henry Miller, *My Life and Times*

La même magie bourgeoise a tous les points
où la malle nous déposera! Le plus élémentaire
physicien sent qu'il n'est plus possible de se
soumettre à cette atmosphère personnelle,
brume de remords physiques, dont la constation
est déjà une affliction.[1]
 —Rimbaud, *Illuminations*

Two remarks by Sigmund Freud, the first from *The Future of an Illusion* (1927): "It goes without saying that a civilization which leaves so large a number of its participants unsatisfied and drives them into revolt neither has nor deserves the prospect of a lasting existence."[2] And the second from *Civilization and Its Discontents* (1930): "Most people do not really want freedom, because freedom involves responsibility, and most people are frightened of responsibility."[3]

What mystified Henry Miller most, I think, is what mystifies any anarchist: Why is it that people so readily consent to be governed? Why do they quietly go to needless wars, or work in degrading jobs, or play out the domestic wars of attrition that, all too often, the conventional nuclear family, stressed to breaking point by financial pressures, ends up becoming, usually through no fault of the unfortunate antagonists? Why do we endure lives of quiet desperation, when we inhabit a world so breathtakingly rich and, in spite, or perhaps because, of its essentially tragic nature, so very beautiful? Why do we not reject the system that controls our everyday lives so rigorously? We are technically free, yes, but only to buy washing powder and to be entertained by whatever garbage we choose from the plethora of garbage available via a wide choice of different media. Why are we so easily fobbed off with cheap substitutes? We want tradition, we get convention; we want sex, we get porn; we want love, we get valentines; we want honor, we get compromise; we want rituals, we get Paroxetine (Paxil). So why do we not *stop* all this? Get out the roller skates. Weigh anchor.

The first answer is that we have been carefully trained to think that there is no other path—not if we wish to be secure (that this security is yet another illusion almost goes without saying). The second answer is to be found in Freud's world-weary remark from 1930: even if we do notice what is happening, the burden of making a real change (even on the "personal" level) will immediately seem immense—that is, immense alongside all the basic maintenance and rendering unto Caesar that we have to deal with day to day. However much harm being governed does to us, to our children, and to our environment, trying to break an entrenched system demands huge reserves of energy, trust, self-confidence, and, at the risk of seeming ridiculous, the "great feeling of love" that, according to Che Guevara, guides the true revolutionary. Not to mention *time*. Had our education been different (had we been raised by wolves, say, or anarchists in the woods), we might feel ready for such a task. But from the age of around eighteen months onward, the Western child is conditioned to live by the clock, to be hungry when he is supposed to be hungry, to sleep, or at least lie down, when Mommy wants her to sleep, to learn this skill and not that, to go to law school when she really wanted to be a dancer—the list goes on and on. We are taught to be creatures of habit; though more often than not, they are somebody else's habits, and not our own. Those habits include voting for people who have no intention whatsoever of representing us in government (how can they, when they owe so much to donors and "friends"?), listening to what a man says because he has (or says he has) money, and believing, after decades of evidence to the contrary, that we can trust what we read in the papers or see on the evening news. They are reprehensible habits all, but when we look around, there isn't a political equivalent to Weight Watchers or A.A. to offer help (it's an appealing thought, though: Voters Anonymous).

We are trained to ignore what our bodies want. We know that each body has its own circadian rhythms, its own needs with regard to sleep and nourishment, its own very particular libido, its own sensory relationships with its environment, its own solitude quotient (the list goes on), but much of what the body wants, what it needs, what would give it a chance of being reasonably *healthy* (even in this industrially polluted world), is at odds with the principal societal schedules based around school and work—the 9 to 5, or 8 till 6, or whatever timetable The Corporation has determined (it is educational, to say the least, to work permanent twelve-hour night shifts at a steel mill, as I once did; this provided, for me, a spectacularly enhanced image of how out of step we can become with our own natural rhythms). Flip through a magazine while you wait for your next doctor's appointment and notice how everything that a contemporary of John Evelyn would have considered a quotidian pleasure—food, sex, drink—has become pathologized. In the nineteenth century we were trained to pretend that we didn't have bodies—even piano legs had to be covered, for fear of exciting lustful thoughts. In my own lifetime, I recall a schoolteacher walking into a classroom where a young woman was combing her hair, and remarking: "Why put that away, Heather! You'll incite the young men!" Now we are trained to study those bodies closely, in order more fully to find fault with them, and to deny ourselves even a moment's physical satisfaction. We are no longer gorgeous parabolas of nervous system, erogenous zones, mind games, and hot-blooded passions; we are medical subjects composed of cholesterol, blood pressure, problematic gonads, and neuroses. In short, we are far too busy being hypochondriacs to upset anybody's apple cart, no matter how rotten—or how polished and waxy and tasteless—the produce may be.

So, as Tolstoy says (and he is still there, at the back of it all, with Luke's Gospel at *his* back, no doubt forever): *What Is to Be Done*? One answer might be found in Henry Miller's short essay, "Peace! It's Wonderful!": "What do I mean to infer? Just this—that art, the art of living, involves the act of creation. The work of art is nothing. It is only the tangible, visible evidence of a way of life, which, if it is not crazy is certainly different from the accepted way of life. The difference lies in the act, in the assertion of a will, and individuality."[4] Several points jump out here. First, that the work of art, the product, is "nothing"—it is like the stone cairn hikers sometimes build when they reach certain points in their walk. It may be good to have the marker, it may be an elegant cairn in itself, but what matters is the walk. Second, Miller identifies the artistic process, not as a practice that happens at the writer's desk, or in the painter's studio, but as "a way of life" that is contrary, in its very essence, to all that the societally accepted way of life intends (a conditioned state that we might call The Authorized Version, a set of prohibitions, false precepts, and bad practices drummed into us by the entire socialization process). Finally, Miller notes that this difference arises from an *act*, and not just an attitude; if the artist—by which, now, he means all of us who dare "the assertion of a will"—is to be an artist *as such*, then she must make her life an act of creation. What she is creating, however, is not just a body of paintings, a book of poems, a career in dance; what she is creating is her true self, liberated from her societally imposed training, the pseudo-education that Miller characterizes as "learning the art of wrestling in order to have the pleasure of letting someone pin you to the mat." The path to this liberation is twofold: the artist must unlearn what she has been taught all her life about being pinned to the mat (that is, she must unlearn how to be governed), and she must then accept the gift that this process delivers as freedom to act as well as freedom to be—and as we know, from another thinker that Miller claimed never to have read, to live and act freely, among others, she must demand the "social scope for the vital manifestation of her being."[5]

In short, she must learn what it means to be an anarchist.

I started to become an anarchist on a train to England at the age of nine. I was staring out of the window at the passing landscape, and for the first time I understood that there was, on the one hand, a natural order that governed everything and, on the other, an order imposed by humans, sometimes for a temporary good (to some humans, at least), though all too often, for ill. Sometimes the natural order and the human *idea* of order converged, or came close to doing so, but this was rare. Many buildings, factories, pastures, and gardens violated the land they occupied, but there were those that *seemed*, at least, in keeping with what could still be seen of the natural terrain. I don't know why I tuned in to this sense of match and mismatch so utterly at that point, and I don't think this sudden vision of order was the result of any great insight on my part. I just turned and looked and something caught my eye, and from that point onward, it all fell into place. It wasn't about liking things that were "natural," or old, or picturesque; it was just a recognition of two different kinds of order. And this is important enough to my overall narrative to repeat: it *really wasn't* about liking something because it was natural (i.e., not human-made) for its own sake because, even then, most of what I was seeing was, if not human-made, then managed by humans to a greater or lesser extent. A devotee of nature books and educational magazines, I knew that pastureland, like copses and drainage systems, had been created by human intervention. I also knew that much of the land we were passing through would once have been forest—originally, the Great Caledonian Forest extended to nigh on four million hectares—so anywhere that wasn't wooded (predominantly with Scots pine) was the result of human intervention. The main point to make is that, even to a child's eye, there was such a clear difference between those interventions that worked with the land, taking their cue and context from it, and those that simply rode roughshod over it.

I saw this and understood it in a child's way as an important fact of life. Less consciously, I also guessed, for the first time, that this was true of everything, including "society," and though I did not use the term "anarchy" at that point, I understood, in a rudimentary way (intuitively, naively) the basic principles of a science—an anarchic knowing—whose main purpose would be to align human behavior as closely as possible to the natural order. At this stage, this nascent understanding did not require a name. However, as time went by and new perceptions and intuitions started to coalesce around those first impressions, they seemed to be moving toward a set of concepts, a coherence, that—child of a taxonomic culture that I was—I wanted more and more to be able to categorize. Politically, partly because of my steel-town upbringing, but mostly because I wasn't actually blind, I was instinctively of the Left (though I balked, from time to time, at the somewhat rigid nature of the good and committed people I was meeting there, people I sometimes suspected of having the same misgivings I had). And yet, as firmly as my immediate circle was red, I was already, and perhaps always had been, inclined to (a very dark) green. Back then, however, the idea that my own way of thinking, a way of thinking that seemed not at all forced or ideological, could be called "anarchism" just did not occur to me. Anarchists were crazy people who threw bombs. Anarchists had strange hair and stranger beards. Anarchists were disorganized. Anarchists were violent (my second-favorite author of that time had written at least one novel about this). Anarchists were too passive—it goes on. The Right laughed at the stock anarchist figure, but the Left mocked him harder and seemed more disturbed by him. Why?

Finally, I got a peek behind the veil. I had long passed the point when I could fool myself into thinking that anything I said or thought was new, so it seemed somebody must have a term for this notion that was fast becoming a way of being in itself, a set of principles that applied to everything, not just politics. A life philosophy, in other words. Surely this notion had its thinkers, its artists, its smiling devotees (though I wasn't sure I needed that last one). Still, the original, rather banal motive for taking that peek behind the veil was a realization that I had, mid-teens, on my way home from a Careers Guidance meeting at my working-class Catholic comprehensive school that the same clumsy and destructive techniques of (mis)management I had seen applied to landscapes, town planning, and "natural resources" were also being applied to me. To the people. Though the file my Careers Officer held in his chubby hand all through our meeting indicated that I had a very high IQ (these things meant something, then) and had come to the school with straight As, it also noted that I was a troubled and troublesome teen, with "difficulties at home" and, no doubt, a "problem with authority." Apparently, I had by then reached a point where nobody wanted to try and fix me, so I was advised to leave school immediately and join the Royal Air Force. This would give me the structure and discipline I needed. What did I think? Was I ready to go out into the world and learn how to operate radar?

As it happened, I didn't need to decide, because I was expelled from that school a few months later and my mother packed me off to Technical College—which was a blessing in disguise. Now I had a library that had real books in it, plenty of time to read, and, as long as I showed my face at more than 50 percent of classes, I could do what I liked. So I read—and my first, accidental discovery was the *Dao De Jing*, which begins with a supremely elegant sidestep to the question that had wastefully consumed hours of my adolescence, namely, "Is there a God?" By then, we were already into the touchy-feely Second Vatican, Age of Aquarius stage of history, a time in which everybody knew that GOD was LOVE, a position I had argued against fiercely as I felt that, if there were a God, then It would, by Its very nature, possess no human attributes, including kindliness, generosity, or gender (i.e., He wasn't a He, or a She, it was an It)—and Love was an attribute, in my book. Now, I had Dao—to Western ears, a nonsense word and, for a necessary transitional period, this was honest: because the Way (the Dao, the Universal Order, Nature, and so on, though none of these terms are adequate) could not be named, it had to remain nameless and, because it could not be described, you couldn't say anything about it. But—and here was the wonderful part—the operations of this unnameable, indescribable Dao (Way) could be observed everywhere in the workings of the natural world, that is, in *physis*, in the "everything that is the case" that made up Being Here, or, to stick with Daoism, in the world of the ten thousand things. If you tried to see Dao, if you were motivated by desire to understand (in itself a kind of will to power), you saw only the illusory; however, if you accepted the natural order and simply observed it—beginning with how it operated in your own body, in the breath, in movement, in thought—then you could apprehend that order *in its workings*. Everywhere you looked, if you looked without the desire to acquire knowledge or "understanding," the law of the Way was inscribed in the movement of the wind, in the flow of water, in how a rock that had stood unchanged for a million years might suddenly crumble at a touch, in all the wide reach of *natura naturans*. And all of this was contained in just the first verse of the *Dao De Jing*. Next came *yin* and *yang*, in the endless cycle of *wuji*—which I got right away, teenage dialectician that I was—in which complementarities arose, like thesis and antithesis, in seeming opposition, only to reconcile, in nature's constant pursuit of a temporary and provisional balance. *Yin* and *yang*, thesis and antithesis—it suddenly became apparent that it was all play, that the world itself was a huge, elegant, and very serious game, a universal balancing act in which the point of equilibrium was constantly shifting.

So—if the Dialectic echoed the principle of *wuji*, what else might Western thought have found to compare with masters like Lao Tse and Chuang Tse? Marx aside, I had lived mostly in the pages of Catholic philosophers like Pascal and the Church Fathers, but after a few false trails and a labored broadening of my horizons, I eventually got to Spinoza: "[M]y argument is this. Nothing comes to pass in nature, which can be set down to a flaw therein; for nature is always the same, and everywhere one and the same in her efficacy and power of action; that is, nature's laws and ordinances, whereby all things come to pass and change from one form to another, are everywhere and always the same; so that there should be one and the same method of understanding the nature of all things whatsoever, namely, through nature's universal laws and rules."[6] Even the Catholics were jumping in there, if I read them carefully enough. For instance, Thomas à Kempis tells us that, if our hearts are right, every living creature is a mirror of life and there is no creature, however, insignificant or ugly that does not reveal the goodness of God,[7] and from there the road meandered dazzlingly through the works of William Godwin, Proudhon, Thoreau, William Morris, Whitman, Emma Goldman, and the various Russian and Italian anarchists who, at times, seemed to get too tied up in a knot arguing about things that didn't matter (God, for example, though I should have seen that their real concern was with the power of various Churches as institutions). Slowly, a worldview began to form in my head, more or less organically and, as it did, it seemed clear that so many questions, and not just the religious one, that I had argued over for years had been irrelevant. What mattered was the discipline of attuning the self to the Way (a lifelong discipline, had I but realized it). And then I found Henry Miller's *other* books—and just as Miller did with Rimbaud, I felt I had discovered something more than a mere influence. (It would be as absurd to be directly influenced by Miller, as it would to be directly influenced by Rimbaud: the point of such writers is not their influence, but how the impossibility of following their example provokes those who come after to their own program of *dérèglement*, their own *fuite*, followed by their own long and disciplined self-recovery/reinvention.)

Miller's work (almost all of it, in fact, though the gist of his anarchism comes over best in compendium books like *The Cosmological Eye*, or *Stand Still Like the Hummingbird*) is a perfect introduction to living (i.e., not-theoretical) anarchism in daily life, partly because, in spite of his love of books, Miller wasn't a book anarchist. He lived it. For him it was natural, instinctive, and had room enough for folly, bouts of intemperance, and all manner of other nonsense, as well as wisdom, discipline, and just measure. Yet, even though he didn't do his spiritual discipline out of a book, he could write it wittily and persuasively, in ways that others could take pages to elucidate and still not express so well (comparable Western commentators might be, on the one hand, Alan Watts, or, coming from another angle altogether, Thomas Merton). Perhaps his greatest gift was the reconciliation, by a kind of poetic means, of glaring paradoxes that any sensible writer with any care for his or her own credibility or reputation would not begin to tolerate. His precinct was the marvelous, the wonderful, the impossible—and he worked it with exemplary good humor.

For example, try explaining to someone who has never engaged with Lao Tse (and a good many who have) what you mean when you use the term *wu wei*. Most people agree it's virtually untranslatable (into English, at least). Whole volumes have been written on the meaning, philosophy, and practice of *wu wei* (and justifiably so), but as an introduction to the idea, these few lines from the aforementioned Miller essay ("Peace! It's Wonderful!") say as much as anyone needs to know (feel), to begin with, at least: "Perhaps just to sit quiet and take deep breathing exercises would be better than popping one another off with slugs of dynamite. Because the strange thing is that just doing nothing, just taking it easy, loafing, meditating, things tend to right themselves." This is good advice, but it should not be misunderstood. *Wu wei*, sometimes translated as "doing by not doing" should not be seen as passive—as quietism or indifference, say. Miller uses the term "sublime indifference," which seems to me a touch combative, but it does give that sense of non-attachment (think Eliot in "Little Gidding," all that live and dead nettle stuff). But I digress. There are many translations of *Dao De Jing*, and it can be hard to find a word that best conveys the idea of *wu wei*, but its opposite is clear, as this translation by Derek Lin shows:

Pursue knowledge, daily gain
Pursue Tao, daily loss
Loss and more loss
Until one reaches unattached action
With unattached action, there is nothing one
   cannot do
Take the world by constantly applying
   non-interference
The one who interferes is not qualified to take
   the world[8]

That's a nice term—"unattached action"—but the key word here is "interference"—which has its many near-synonyms in the modern world (our grim obsession with illusions of "progress" and "development" being the most insidious). As Miller says, with obvious scorn for meddlers everywhere, "the whole damned universe has to be taken apart, brick by brick, and reconstructed. Every atom has to be rearranged." Why? Because we always want to improve on everything (especially "Nature"). Because we love the idea of "Progress." Or is it just because development brings money to those who already have more than enough? (We all know that, if you have sufficient for the day, then you can't be a developer, no matter what any developer tells you. You have to possess collateral of some kind, or the banks don't loan you money. Or, as Miller says elsewhere, "To do anything, you need money"—including, it seems, the making of money.)

The essence of Miller's anarchism, then, is drawn as much from Daoist philosophy as from writers we would usually think of as anarchists—that is, "political" anarchists—and the reason he has been misunderstood, as an anarchist, is the same reason why anarchism itself has been misunderstood (very often with cool deliberation) throughout its history. For, just as Daoism has been represented as a religion by the religious, so anarchism has been represented as an ideology by the political. Anarchists are also denigrated by the "realists" in political and social life (on both the Left and the Right), that is, by those who say, smugly, that politics is the art of the possible. In recent years, however, we have come to a point where the possible—or at least, the possible as defined by our self-designated realists—is not enough to prevent us from damaging our environment so utterly that it is no longer livable. What we need now is a commitment to what realists think of as *impossible*—in human terms, at least. Besides, as Miller knew all too well, the possible is not an art; it's just a defense mechanism for those who aren't brave enough to trust in the natural order.

At the same time, Miller recognizes that joining political parties is, in itself, counterproductive.

"To get men to rally round a cause, a belief, an idea, is always easier than to persuade them to lead their own lives," he says, in "An Open Letter to Surrealists Everywhere," and he continues:

The role which the artist plays in society is to revive the primitive, anarchic instincts which have been sacrificed for the illusion of living in comfort. If the artist fails we will not necessarily have a return to an imaginary Eden filled with wonder and cruelty. I am afraid, on the contrary, that we are much more apt to have a condition of perpetual work, such as we see in the insect world. Myself I do not believe that the artist will fail. On the other hand, it doesn't matter a damn to me whether he fails or not. It is a problem beyond my scope. If I choose to remain an artist rather than go down in the street and shoulder a musket or sling a stick of dynamite it is because my life as an artist suits me down to the ground. It is not the most comfortable life in the world but I know that it is life, and I am not going to trade it for an anonymous life in the brotherhood of man— which is either sure death, or quasi-death, or at the very best cruel deception. I am fatuous enough to believe that in living my own life in my own way I am more apt to give life to others (though even that is not my chief concern) than I would if I simply followed somebody else's idea of how to live my life and thus become a man among men. It seems to me that this struggle for liberty and justice is a confession or admission on the part of all those engaging in such a struggle that they have failed to live their own lives.[9]

Reading Miller, we see again and again that his anarchism is based upon the first precept of anarchist philosophy, which is that order resides in the natural world, and that the artist/anarchist discovers that order by studying the world around him—*as well as his own, individual nature*—with unflinching discipline. This, in fact, is the true work of the artist: and the careful reader may well come to feel that Miller uses the terms "artist" and "anarchist" almost interchangeably, partly because both must learn to become fully spontaneous in order to be. "Through art," he says, "one finally establishes contact with reality: that is the great discovery. Here all is play and invention; there is no solid foothold from which to launch the projectiles which will pierce the miasma of folly, ignorance and greed. The world has not to be put in order: the world is order incarnate. It is for us to put ourselves in unison with this order, to know what is the world order in contradistinction to the wishful-thinking orders which we seek to impose on one another."[10] This is the key, the source idea, for both disciplines. Yet commentators and critics all too often ignore, or downplay the centrality of this precept to Miller's worldview. Wallace Fowlie, for example, attaches Miller's "personal creed" (i.e., faith, ideology) "in part to the European utopia of the noble savage, and in part to the American tradition of return to nature we read in Thoreau and Whitman. His sense of anarchy is partly that of Thoreau and partly that of the Beat Generation."[11]

Now, this is not only to diminish Miller, but also to diminish Thoreau. By placing Thoreau in an American tradition of "return to nature," Fowlie forgets his activism, his support of direct action against slavery, and the fact that he composed *Civil Disobedience*, one of the most important texts of resistance ever written, the handbook of Gandhi, Martin Luther King Jr., and many others. He forgets that Thoreau did not disappear into the woods around Walden Pond to fish or whittle twigs, but spent his two years there learning how to live fully: "I went to the woods because I wished to live deliberately, to front only the essential facts of life, and see if I could not learn what it had to teach, and not, when I came to die, discover that I had not lived." After two years, having acquired at least some of the "essential facts of life," mostly by observing the workings of the natural world, he *returned* to the societal sphere and resumed his work against injustice and a property-based system so corrupted that it could even treat human life as a commodity. In short, Thoreau did not go to the woods to "return to nature," simply: his was an act of *la fuite*, a setting forth into the unknown terrain, not of Walden, but of his own mind and spirit. In the same way, Henry Miller did not leave America to live the boho life in Paris, as so many did; he abandoned everything and sailed away, with ten dollars in his pocket, to become the writer he wanted—needed—to be.

Fowlie is not alone, however, in his casual underestimation of Miller's belief system—for in truth, no set of ideas has ever been more carefully denigrated and willfully misrepresented than the bundle of interlinked philosophical precepts that true anarchists espouse. It is said that anarchists are "violent," even though the use of violence, as such, is contrary to the *wu wei* principle of acting in accordance with the natural order. But let us be careful here. The first thing to define while having this conversation is "violence" itself, and that is not a simple matter. When Emma Goldman says, "Ask for work. If they don't give you work, ask for bread. If they do not give you work or bread, then take bread," is she advocating violence?[12] What she describes here seems entirely reasonable, even from the point of view of a property-based society: what she is saying is exactly what the homemade cardboard placard held by the homeless person says today on too many city streets: WILL WORK FOR FOOD. But if you refuse me work, and also refuse me bread, what am I to do? As Gandhi was known to remark: "Poverty is [also] violence." When you have food and shelter and money and all the goods you need, if not everything you covet, and you deprive me of a meal, then you are doing violence to me and to those I care for. As a living creature, I will instinctively seek food and shelter; as a father or a mother, I have a duty to feed my children. In short, if you hoard all the bread, and will not even let me work for a little of it, then I have no choice but to take it. This is the principle that always applies in a property-based society. In an anarchist community, however (which is not based on property, hierarchy, and inequality), there can be no question of hoarding, because nothing, other than a range of personal items and, at any one time, a place of shelter, belongs exclusively to a single individual, or group. We work together, we eat together. Each contributes as she can. From each according to his abilities, to each according to his needs. The man who cures your ailments and the woman who builds your public buildings (if you have any); the family who grow quality food, and the family who run the local bookshop; the solitary painter in his attic studio and the storyteller who enchants the entire community with tales of origin and mystery; the cleaner and the gardener, the carpenter and the actor, the mechanic and the fisherman—all have an equal place in this community. "We all derive from the same source," Miller says. "There is no mystery about the origin of things. We are all part of creation, all kings, all poets, all musicians; we have only to open up, to discover what is already there."[13]

Like a Fluid (The Great Romantic)

The great artist is he who conquers the romantic in himself.

—Henry Miller, *Black Spring*

He loved the trees he had played under as a boy as if they were living creatures; that was on the romantic side of his nature. Merely looking at them as representing so many pounds sterling, he had esteemed them highly, and had had, until now, no opinion of another by which to correct his own judgment. So these words of the valuers cut him sharp, although he affected to disbelieve them, and tried to persuade himself that he did so. But, after all, these cares and disappointments did not touch the root of his deep resentment against Osborne. There is nothing like wounded affection for giving poignancy to anger. And the squire believed that Osborne and his advisers had been making calculations, based upon his own death. He hated the idea so much—it made him so miserable—that he would not face it, and define it, and meet it with full inquiry and investigation.

—Elizabeth Gaskell, *Wives and Daughters*

It comes as a surprise to remember that each of us witnesses small-scale tragedies every day. The colleague I once had, who drank himself into an early grave, who knew exactly what was happening, but could do nothing to stop it, just as we— his friends, his family, his beautiful and intelligent young wife—could do nothing to save him. The battered wife who conceals her injuries and her humiliations and all those around her who go along with the deception. The gifted musician who cannot find the audience that might appreciate her gifts, watching television as "stars" are created instantly on screen via a combination of audiovisual trickery, clever makeup, and public relations. Or simply the grinding down of our parents by an industrial society—something I recall now, forty years after the event, so fiercely that it still smarts.

We have become accustomed to tolerating such things—and yet, if these were not enough, we also allow our hearts to be broken, now and then, by a shred of fiction, or a passing incident in what, for others, is an altogether different tale. My first memory of this self-betrayal comes from a Sunday afternoon in the 1960s, when I first saw the film *Lawrence of Arabia*, an account that I knew was not altogether "historically accurate." What got to me most wasn't even an important event; it was a passing moment in the scene where Peter O'Toole, as T. E. Lawrence, comes into the officer's club with a young Arab boy and the Englishmen are shocked and offended because he's brought a bloody native into their holy place. They are, in fact, on the point of throwing both these interlopers out when O'Toole says, with pride and defiance: "We have taken Aqaba." However, what I wanted to know was: what happened next? something I couldn't know, because the director cut away here and left me guessing. Did David Lean not know that I—or somebody in the audience, at least—didn't care about Aqaba, that I only cared about what happened to the boy? Did that brave child get his glass of ice water? Or did the staff force him out, while Lawrence stayed on to tell his larger story? I had a hero-complex about Lawrence, even then, because I believed that people like him *knew*, as I knew, that you can win any battle you like, but you still can't be in the club. It's not about talent, it's not about worth. It's about who is allowed to be in the club and who isn't. As it happens, you don't want to be in the club, you even despise the club, but you also can't stand it that the people who belong to the club get to control everything. You rally thousands of men to your cause, you take Aqaba and the other tactical prizes, and then, after all the promises you have made, in good faith, the people in the club turn up where the real business gets done (in London, in Paris, in Versailles) and betray every decent principle the warrior class is supposed to uphold—the first and foremost being honor. And the Arab boy probably doesn't get his glass of ice water, either.

Somewhere between the fictional sources of grief and the societal, lies the domain where husbands and wives take the field. Each comes armed with a fantasy of what marriage could be and, for one partner, if not for the other, a sense of what can and should be settled for. One of the most poignant passages in Henry Miller's writing is this one, from *The World of Sex*, in which he pictures an alliance of two souls in wedlock that he himself never achieves, but goes on hoping for, at some level, into his final years:

> Once I saw a picture of Rubens as he looked when he married his young wife. They were portrayed together, he standing beside or behind her as she sat for the portrait. I shall never forget the emotion it inspired in me. I had one long deep look into the world of contentment, a world of mutual understanding, of love, of mature bliss. I felt the vigor of Rubens, then in the prime of his life; I felt the confidence which he breathed in the presence of his very young

wife. I felt that some great event had occurred and had been fixed on canvas for eternity. I do not know the story of his life, whether he lived happily ever afterwards with her or not. I don't care what happened subsequently. *I care about that moment which was true and inspiring.* I saw it only a few seconds, but it will remain with me, imperishable.[1] (my italics)

We can, of course, argue that this is a dream, an image from a work of art. But is it really so? For a moment, a man who married five times had a vision of what marriage could be. The only difference between that vision and the lived reality is *time*. We, who live in this world, consider a marriage a failure if it does not last: if it ends after five years, seven years, even twenty. It is supposed to be happy ever after. We know that's an absurd notion, and yet we choose to live with the cognitive dissonance. Yet what if we reversed the whole "vision" and called any marriage happy, if it achieved just one moment like the one Rubens and his young wife are enjoying in the picture? If, when the couple parts, five, or seven, or twenty years later, it can pride itself on this fleeting moment—and the others that were like it? Rainer Maria Rilke has a poem, *Ehe* (Marriage) in which he talks of a not entirely unrelated vision of married love:

Hundertmal in deiner dumpfen Gier
warst du ihr Vergeuder und Vergifter;
aber daß du einmal wie ein Stifter
still und dunkel knietest neben ihr
macht dich männlich und geht aus von dir.

(A hundred times, in your dull greed
you have squandered and poisoned her;
but once, you knelt alongside her,
dark and silent, like a donor
this makes you manly, and goes out from you.)[2]

With that coupling of *Vergeuder* and *Vergifter*, this is an astonishing, harsh passage (and it demands a more detailed reading than there is space for here), but that moment of true manliness at the close, in which the male becomes dark and silent, a kneeling donor honoring what is good in both partners, may just be the counter to the false ideas of manliness that Miller's generation—and mine, in somewhat altered form—grew up with. Is it possible, however, for a man to rise to this condition of "donor," and, if so, can that condition survive the woe that is in marriage?

There is a passage in *The Colossus of Maroussi* that has haunted, and troubled, me ever since I first read it, decades ago. It is a passing moment, no more, a few lines to describe a fleeting vision of a young girl on a street in Athens, but it stuck in my mind then, and, returning to it today, I am struck by its beauty, and by how disturbing I still find it:

> How can I ever forget the young girl whom we passed one day at the foot of the Acropolis? Perhaps she was ten, perhaps she was fourteen years of age; her hair was reddish gold, her features as noble, as grave and austere as those of the caryatids on the Erectheum. She was playing with some comrades in a little clearing before a clump of ramshackle shanties which had somehow escaped the general demolition. Anyone who has read *Death in Venice* will appreciate my sincerity when I say that no woman, not even the loveliest woman I have ever seen, is or was capable of arousing in me such a feeling of adoration as this young girl elicited. *If Fate were to put her in my path again I know not what folly I might commit.* She was child, virgin, angel, seductress, priestess, harlot, prophetess all in one.[3] (my italics)

What is Miller saying here? Could he write such a passage now? Would he? And is there a real moral question to be raised with regard to its content or *is everything permitted to the imagination*?

Two things about this passage make it seriously problematic: first, that *it is not fiction*, and second, that, while it is a hymn to beauty in its nearly perfect human form, a spiritual pronouncement reminiscent of Dante, Thomas Mann, and others, it is also, in some real measure, *sexual*. In short, it is a confession of desire for a girl who could be as young as ten. True, this is neither Humbert Humbert drooling over some nymphet, nor Lewis Carroll at the seaside with his pocketful of safety pins (he used them to strike up "friendships" with young girls who wanted to paddle in the waves but were encumbered by their long skirts). Nevertheless, it is unsettling to read. But why? Beatrice was only twelve years old when Dante first saw her, so whatever evil motive we might ascribe to Miller we must also ascribe to Dante. Either that, or we have to concede that there is no such thing as "spiritual love."

At the same time, the figure Miller is describing is not the forbidden love from the days of his youth (that is, not the girl with the violet eyes he remembers, both from his own, and also from Rimbaud's youth) because, in truth, it is more abstract and, at the same time, more real, than "something with a girl in summer," as Robert Lowell puts it. This could sound dismissive, but Lowell knows, as Miller knows, that *she* exists, always and everywhere, as a potential presence— and every other lover is an instance, more or less, of an approximation of that impossible ideal. *She* cannot be held, she cannot be married, she cannot stay—for, as beautiful as she is, she is also a near-cousin to death, *your* death, personal death. If you see her on the street, and follow her, she will evade you, at least for a time; if you persist, she will take the dark stairway that leads down to the river, where who knows what might step out to greet you—and if you think cousin death is the worst of the possibilities, then this is clearly your first time at the dark end of the fair. She is perfect, and she is impossible—and the only thing you know for sure is that, if you see her out walking on a moonlit night, you do well to stop and watch her pass.

On rare occasions when two people meet and each recognizes in the other this extreme romantic temperament, they proceed to make an exquisite game of the encounter, a game in which anything is possible, even touch. It goes without saying, however, that the outcome of this play cannot be predicted: it may end in exquisite pain or exquisite beauty, but the one imperative is that it remain a game, for as long as it lasts. Any attempt to make it last beyond its natural span, any attempt to incorporate it into everyday life, any attempt to cling, to hold on, will reduce it to an unbearable banality. The great romantic learns that one must reject anything that is societally possible and pledge oneself to the impossible—and it may seem perverse to say so, but is it not possible that this passage finally blows Miller's cover and reveals him, not as the sly pornographer, or as the Frank Harris wannabe, but as one of the great romantics? No doubt the jury is still out on that, but I like the thought of leaving it there and remembering that, while there is still breath, there is still hope—even for husbands and wives. All we need do is forget the societal standard for what makes a successful marriage and celebrate the many forms of success that couples achieve, on their way from one life stage to another. It's a fine thing to imagine: the divorce party, where friends and former loves raise a glass to send the parting spouses on their way, without bitterness and with no sense of "failure" (and no wrangling about who "gets" what), to the next adventure in the search for one more instance of the impossible.

The Air-Conditioned Nightmare

> It is a world suited for monomaniacs obsessed with the idea of progress—but a false progress, a progress which stinks.
>
> —Henry Miller, *The Air-Conditioned Nightmare*

> Why should we tolerate a diet of weak poisons, a home in insipid surroundings, a circle of acquaintances who are not quite our enemies, the noise of motors with just enough relief to prevent insanity? Who would want to live in a world which is just not quite fatal?
>
> —Rachel Carson, *Silent Spring*

Two outstanding works mark the highest point of Henry Miller's career and, though they were both travel books of a sort, they could not be more unlike. The first, *The Colossus of Maroussi*, a hymn to Greece under the shadow of war, was published by Colt Press in 1941. The second, *The Air-Conditioned Nightmare*, a jeremiad on the folly, ugliness, and injustices of the United States, appeared first in 1945, when America was at its most triumphalist. As always, Miller's timing was execrable—and oddly heroic.

By now, Miller knew what he was about: he had identified the enemies of freedom, not only in high places, but also in the family home, the registrar's office, the pharmacy, the police station, and the bedroom. Any person who has been subjected to sustained societal conditioning is potentially an agent of the state. This is true of men who collaborate with the state to limit the experience and potential of their wives and daughters, but it is also true of women who do the same things—by different means—to their husbands and sons. The recruiting sergeant, banging about town with his press gang is no more heinous than the well-dressed society lady with her purse full of white feathers. A woman like Henry Miller's mother may appear less contemptible than a violent husband, but she gets the job done, nevertheless.

Like many of us who are badly treated in childhood—collateral damage, more often than not, in the war between the man and the woman— Miller took years to recover. Some never do. We have to remember that what he was trying to protect and sustain was more than just a sense of his own masculinity; it was personhood itself. In a society that enlists mother, father, wife, husband, children, colleagues, sporting heroes, and pageant queens to limit the imaginative freedom of its citizenry, Miller was struggling for the right to govern himself and to not be manipulated by his society. In an age when most people actively coveted the new "gewgaws," or at least saw them as innocent enough, Miller did not want to live in a consumerist society, and he dared to name it for what it was, at a time when imperialist booster-ism was at its height.

Obliged to leave Paris in 1939, Miller had accepted a long-standing invitation to visit Lawrence Durrell in Greece (the Durrells were living in Corfu). Not only did he visit, he spent nine months there wandering about the country, using Athens and the Durrells' home as his bases, visiting Poros, Phaestos, Mycenae, Crete, and Delphi and, through the "Colossus" of the title, George Katsimbalis, met the poet George Seferis and the painter Ghika (Nikos Hadjikyriakos-Ghikas). What changed Miller, however—what made him grow as a writer—was his encounter with the land itself:

It was a voyage into the light. The earth became illumined by her own inner light. At Mycenae I walked over the incandescent dead; at Epidaurus I felt a stillness so intense that for a fraction of a second I heard the great heart of the world beat and I understood the meaning of pain and sorrow; at Tiryns I stood in the shadow of the Cyclopean man and felt the blaze of that inner eye which has not become a sickly gland; at Argos the whole plain was a fiery mist in which I saw the ghosts of our own American Indians and greeted them in silence.[1]

There can be no overestimating the impact of Greece on Miller's imagination—or his craft. Most important, it seems to have enriched his philosophy in ways that all the reading and conversations in Paris and New York could never have done. Now, he says, he has become "one with the Path"; now, "The Greek earth opens before me like the Book of Revelation. I never knew that the earth contains so much: I had walked blindfolded, with faltering, hesitant steps; I was proud and arrogant, content to live the false, restricted life of the city man. The light of Greece opened my eyes, penetrated my pores, expanded my whole being. I came home to the world, having found the true center and the real meaning of revolution."[2]

However, as he also notes, Greece was "becoming embroiled" in the war and, now that the whole of Europe was similarly embroiled, it seemed, after those halcyon nine months, that there was only one place for Miller to go. He may have felt, in Greece, that he was coming "home to the world," but circumstances dictated that he now return to the place he claimed to detest more than any other—and it was there, in New York, while avoiding his parents and asking friends to keep his whereabouts unknown, that Miller wrote *The Colossus of Maroussi*, perhaps his happiest, certainly his brightest, and, in the eyes of many, himself included, probably the best of his books.

As soon as he was done with it, however, he started thinking about the book that would *seem* to be its polar opposite: a vitriolic, merciless, and, at times, insanely funny attack, not just on America itself, but on the way the entire "developed" world was going. As he traveled across the United States, doing the "research" that would inform *The Air-Conditioned Nightmare*, Miller became convinced that "nowhere else in the world is the divorce between man and nature so complete. Nowhere have I encountered such a dull, monotonous fabric of life as here. . . . Here boredom reaches its peak."[3] Did he know, then, that, within a decade or so, the rest of the "developed" world, even France and Greece, would follow? In the preface to *The Air-Conditioned Nightmare*, Miller claims that the thought of "writing a book on America" had come to him in Paris "some years ago," but he didn't begin work, proper, until 1941, owing to lack of funds ("To do anything you need money,' he remarks, as if somehow surprised by the fact) and an unfamiliarity with the American highway (throughout the book, Miller's ineptitude, not only as a mechanic, but also as a driver, provides a running source of hilarity, especially toward the end of the journey, when he limps across the deserts of the Southwest in a car he was clearly far from qualified to drive in such conditions). Yet, even when he got on the road, he couldn't write a line, so horrified was he by the return to his homeland, and it took a good deal of mental fight before the book was finally published in 1945, by New Directions.

It almost goes without saying that, if there was ever a bad year to publish a biting critique of American life, it was 1945. Emerging from what the majority felt was a just war as the most powerful nation on earth (and with the world's first-ever weapons of mass destruction to strengthen his hand), Harry S. Truman probably felt that he spoke for all when he told Congress, in January 1946, that the previous year had been "*the greatest year of achievement in human history*. It saw the end of the Nazi-Fascist terror in Europe, and also the end of the malignant power of Japan. And it saw the substantial beginning of world organization for peace. . . . *The plain fact is that civilization was saved in 1945* by the United Nations" (my italics).

Then, having paid tribute to "the millions of Americans" both military and civilian, who had worked together to achieve what many would soon recognize, not as a victory for the United Nations, but a *Pax Americana*, he continued: "The beginning of the year 1946 finds the United States strong and deservedly confident. We have a record of enormous achievements as a democratic society in solving problems and meeting opportunities as they developed. We find ourselves possessed of immeasurable advantages—vast and varied natural resources; great plants, institutions, and other facilities; unsurpassed technological and managerial skills; an alert, resourceful, and able citizenry. We have in the United States Government rich resources in information, perspective, and facilities for doing whatever may be found necessary to do in giving support and form to the widespread and diversified efforts of all our people."[4]

The rhetoric is familiar, of course; but at the end of World War II, it seems likely that more ordinary working people took it at face value than at any other time in American history. Certainly, it was not the best moment for Miller to announce that, in spite of his intention to travel his former homeland "with a blessing on my lips," his initial impression, when he got off the boat in Boston, was that this homeland had become a "vast jumbled waste created by pre-human or sub-human monsters in a delirium of greed"—and, if that wasn't insult enough, continuing just a page or so later: "Maybe we would end up on all fours, gibbering like baboons. Something disastrous was in store—everybody felt it. Yes, America had changed. The lack of resilience, the feeling of hopelessness, the resignation, the skepticism, the defeatism—I could scarcely believe my ears at first. And over it all the same veneer of fatuous optimism—only now decidedly cracked." And just in case any doubt remained, he presses further: "A new world is not made simply by trying to forget the old. A new world is made with a new spirit, with new values. Our world may have begun that way, but today it is a caricature. Our world is a world of things. It is made up of comforts and luxuries, or else the desire for them. What we dread most, in facing the impending debacle, is that we shall be obliged to give up our gewgaws, our gadgets, all the little comforts which have made us so uncomfortable. There is nothing brave, chivalrous, heroic or magnanimous about our attitude. We are not peaceful souls; we are smug, timid, queasy and quakey."[5] There is no sense of suspense in *The Air-Conditioned Nightmare*; before the reader is a dozen pages into the book, she knows that America is rotten to the core, a sham, run by greedy, venial, smug men whose only values are based on property and status, men who would sell anything—the land, their souls, their history—to anyone who cared to bid for them.

At the same time, the book is full of surprises. One of my favorite chapters is the surreal "Letter to Lafayette," in which nothing is explained and there is no background to any of the characters (John Dudley, a painter from Kenosha, whom Miller had met at Caresse Crosby's house in Bowling Green while working on *The Colossus of Maroussi*; Dudley's wife, Flo; and a writer named Lafayette, or Lafe Young, who was to become a friend and associate of Charles Bukowski). All we know is that Dudley and Young had been trying to start a magazine, *Generation*, that it had failed, and now Lafe was off somewhere, while Dudley set about composing a book-length letter to him that would encapsulate the concerns of their generation: "I want to wash up my own life and literature too. The book opens with a nightmare, an evacuation, *a complete waste of images.*" Dudley also speaks of wandering "through jungles, rivers, swamps, deserts—in search of the Mayas. We are trying to find our father, our name, our address." Meanwhile Lafe writes nihilistic letters from Des Moines, full of hermetic phrases and declarations: "It'll all be blue. I demit. I abdicate. I renounce," prompting Miller to note: "Most of

the young men of talent I have met in this country give one the impression of being somewhat
demented. Why shouldn't they? They are living
amidst spiritual gorillas, living with food and
drink maniacs, success-mongers, gadget inno-
vators, publicity hounds. God, if I were a young
man today, if I were faced with a world such as
we have created, I would blow my brains out."[6]

"A complete waste of images," "trying to find
our father, our name, our address"—it's all so
reminiscent of Kerouac and Cassidy and even Jim
Morrison, driving back and forth across America
(before *On the Road* gets written and—finally,
after years—becomes the product America
uses to kill Kerouac off, slowly, turning on him
the light of the public that darkens everything).
A new, wholly American variety of *la fuite*, in
which the land, freed of the burden of landscape,
or home place, and in that fleeting blessed state
before the developers got properly to work, *becomes* time. Which is to say, it becomes a terrain
in which history can be avoided, all the conclu-
sions staved off, a space for demission, for renun-
ciation, for the holy abdication of a Rimbaud.
Meanwhile, back at the ranch—but there it was in
all its drabness. There was the problem: nobody
is back at the ranch. It may even be the case that
the ranch itself is gone, lost long ago in a poker
game with the ghost of Wild Bill Hickok, or, like

as not, in some Wall Street Ponzi scheme. No-body stayed back to say: Let's keep it minimal, boys. It's not cool, here—not yet—to hang loose and say nothing, and it's certainly not okay to give up and play the real-world game with a shrug to show that you see the irony of all this, but what else can you do, you'll never win? No: Lafe and Dudley "look at their fathers and grandfathers, all brilliant successes in the world of American flapdoodle. They prefer to be shit-heels, if they have to be."[7] Anyway, it's not about winning. Or it wasn't then. Now, I'm not so sure—now all you need is front, but it's not cool and it's not ironic at all if you never even tried for Being Beaute-ous. You begin and end with the pose, and after a token period of black crepe or Jungian analysis you opt for two automobiles and your own home with a pipe organ in it.

It is odd, looking back, to think that, in the 1940s and '50s, America was full of Lafes and Dudleys (and Kerouacs, and Bukowskis, and Cassidys) but nobody knew it. It probably is now, or if not, it probably has its fair share of boys like Coyd Jr. from Rodney Jones's poem "The As-sault on the Fields." A teenage pop singer and artist from a newly electrified holler somewhere down in the deep, late 1950s South, living blithely under the "rolling boil" of DDT (the deposits get so thick, his sister Jenny uses them to draw hopscotch lines), Coyd paints his own abstract expressionist works, inspired by the works of Joel Shapiro; his pride and joy is a black canvas in a black frame:

"I call it *Death*," he would say,
then stomp out onto the front lawn to shoot
    his .22 rifle
straight into the sky above his head[8]

—oh, what energy and infantry training America expended on containing its young folk! Meanwhile, it was already busy poisoning everything else—and that would lead to the wide, and entirely unwanted public prominence of another kind of writer, but one with a great deal in common with Henry Miller, if not John Dudley and Lafayette Young.

Some years ago, on the fortieth anniversary of *Silent Spring* (first published in the *New Yorker* in 1962), I got together with poet and *experienced* anthologist Maurice Riordan and persuaded him to help me put a book out on the fortieth anniversary of Carson's death in 2004. A week or so after, he reluctantly agreed (unlike me, he knew what putting an anthology together actually involved). Maurice, a generous-hearted Irish poet with social skills I have only read about in magazines, left me in a bar while he trooped off to a meeting with the Gulbenkian Foundation; by the time he got back, we had guaranteed publication and a significant sum of cash to commission new work from some of our favorite contemporary poets (to this day, I still have no idea how such things are done). The outcome of this project was a book called *Wild Reckoning*, an anthology of poems chosen from several centuries of what I was then calling "eco-critical" poetry, alongside twenty new works by poets as diverse as Mark Doty and Seamus Heaney, Andrew Motion and Allison Funk. One idea of the book was that the commissioned work would arise (spontaneously, and organically, we hoped) from an exchange—a lunch, a working meeting, a conversation—between our poet and a working scientist and, while some poets preferred to go their own way for inspiration, some of the best work was clearly informed by those meetings of two minds. The anthology did well and went into several editions; it was a Poetry Book Society Special Commendation and (my favorite of its badges of honor) was the book choice on *Desert Island Discs* of the UK government's chief scientific adviser and surface chemistry pioneer, Sir David King.

I have written elsewhere on Carson, in an attempt to draw attention to her work in *The Sea Trilogy*, and I consider myself her Number One Fan—and, as my youngest son would say, *I mention all this why*? Well, mainly so it does not seem "negative," or unfairly critical, or just petty-minded when I say that, contrary to the accepted wisdom, the modern environmental movement did not begin with *Silent Spring*, in spite of all arguments to the contrary (see, e.g., Peter Matthiessen in *Time* magazine, March 29, 1999: "Before there was an environmental movement, there was one brave woman and her very brave book."). To say so would be to fail to appreciate the work of any number of her predecessors and contemporaries: Aldo Leopold, say, whose *A Sand County Almanac: And Sketches Here and There* was published in 1949; or Edwin Way Teale who, in the 1930s and '40s, was already at work transforming the lay American reader's vision of the natural world; or Loren Eiseley who, in 1957, wrote the one sentence on the living world that I most wish I had written: "There is no logical reason for the existence of a snowflake any more than there is for evolution. It is an apparition from that mysterious shadow world beyond nature, that final world which contains—if anything contains—the explanation of men and catfish and green leaves"[9]—but in truth the line goes way back, through Victorian writers like John Lubbock to William Cobbett (who, in 1825, said of the new mills at Chilworth, "here has the devil fixed on as one of the seats of his grand manufactory; and perverse and ungrateful man not only lends him his aid, but lends it cheerfully!").[10] In fact, it could be argued that the first book to deliver a sustained "eco-critical" examination of the damage being done by modern capitalist industrial processes, not only to our environment, but to ourselves, predates *Silent Spring* by a hundred years. That book was George Perkins Marsh's *Man and Nature: Or, Physical Geography as Modified by Human Action* (it was first published in 1864, and in a revised edition in 1874). In many ways, it could be argued that Marsh was, in fact, the first modern environmentalist, certainly in America.

Occasional critiques by poets and others go back further still, certainly to the German and English Romantics, but, for me, the case against the industrialization of daily life is most eloquently expressed in the writings of William Morris, who saw that the machine-age paradigm was not only polluting the land and the atmosphere, but also the souls of those who had to live in such degraded conditions. Here he is, for example, in a speech titled "Hopes and Fears for Art," given before the Trades' Guild of Learning, on December 4, 1877:

> And Science—we have loved her well, and followed her diligently, what will she do? I fear she is so much in the pay of the counting-house, the counting-house and the drill-sergeant,

that she is too busy, and will for the present do nothing. Yet there are matters which I should have thought easy for her; say for example teaching Manchester how to consume its own smoke, or Leeds how to get rid of its superfluous black dye without turning it into the river, which would be as much worth her attention as the production of the heaviest of heavy black silks, or the biggest of useless guns. Anyhow, however it be done, unless people care about carrying on their business without making the world hideous, how can they care about Art? . . . Unless something or other is done to give all men some pleasure for the eyes and rest for the mind in the aspect of their own and their neighbours' houses, until the contrast is less disgraceful between the fields where beasts live and the streets where men live, I suppose that the practice of the arts must be mainly kept in the hands of a few highly cultivated men, who can go often to beautiful places, whose education enables them, in the contemplation of the past glories of the world, to shut out from their view the everyday squalors that the most of men move in. Sirs, I believe that art has such sympathy with cheerful freedom, open-heartedness and reality, so much she sickens under selfishness and luxury, that she will not live thus isolated and exclusive. I will go further than this and say that on such terms I do not wish her to live. I protest that it would be a shame to an honest artist to enjoy what he had huddled up to himself of such art, as it would be for a rich man to sit and eat dainty food amongst starving soldiers in a beleaguered fort . . . I do not want art for a few, any more than education for a few, or freedom for a few.[11]

It would, of course, be convenient for the captains of industry and finance, if the environmental movement *had* begun with *Silent Spring* (and if it had only been about DDT, or even pesticides, rather than the innate corruption running throughout an entire system), but I am sure Carson would have been the first to say otherwise. This is important because those in power didn't just ignore her holistic perspective on the natural world; they have consistently ignored warnings that, year upon year, decade upon decade, have been sounded, and proven, by generation after generation of dissenters. From the first indications that "developed" societies were moving toward the industrialization of everything (including culture, including *scientia*, including life itself), dissident voices have been raised and, even if those voices have been varied, all of them—Spinoza, Goethe, Samuel Taylor Coleridge, John Clare, R.W.

Emerson, H. D. Thoreau, William Morris, D. H. Lawrence, Martin Heidegger, and many, many others—have offered the same warnings. We are gaining the world, materially, but losing whatever it is that constitutes the soul. We are sacrificing our place in the natural order, to dwell in a vast, ugly, and rather cheaply constructed machine. We are losing the other animals. We are accepting it as an inevitability that, as Emerson points out, "every actual state is corrupt" and so failing in our duties of citizenly vigilance. We are making cynicism and cowardice into fashion statements. Worse, we are living in the condition that Cornel West has defined thus: "Nihilism is a natural consequence of a culture (or civilization) ruled and regulated by categories that mask manipulation, mastery and domination of peoples and nature."[12] Not to acknowledge this is a profound failure in critical thinking. Since the end of World War II, however, with the rewriting, or erasure, of much of our history in "developed" countries—and most of all in America—to point this out in a public forum is considered "negative," defeatist, and unpatriotic.

The focus, and the methods, of *The Air-Conditioned Nightmare* and *Silent Spring* are, of course, quite different, but both Miller and Carson attack the same problems. Sometimes, indeed, I can hear their voices merging, as if one. For example, who is speaking here?

The question is whether any civilization can wage relentless war on life without destroying itself, and without losing the right to be called civilized.

And here?

We tell the story as though man were an innocent victim, a helpless participant in the erratic and unpredictable revolutions of Nature. Perhaps in the past he was. But not any longer. Whatever happens to this earth today is of man's doing. Man has demonstrated that he is master of everything—except his own nature. If yesterday he was a child of nature, today he is a responsible creature. He has reached a point of consciousness which permits him to lie to himself no longer.

Here?

The earth is not a lair, neither is it a prison. The earth is a Paradise, the only one we'll ever know. We will realize it the moment we open our eyes. We don't have to make it a Paradise—it is one. We have only to make ourselves fit to inhabit it.

And here?

This is an era of specialists, each of whom sees his own problem and is unaware of or intolerant of the larger frame into which it fits. It is also an era dominated by industry, in which the right to make a dollar at whatever cost is seldom challenged.[13]

There is too much in *The Air-Conditioned Nightmare* to touch on all of it in such a short space. Because it is so critical of the United States, it is less popular with a certain sector of readers than it might have been, which is a pity, because Miller's real target was not so much America as a spirit of vapid consumerism that was bound to disgust someone who "had the misfortune to be nourished by the dreams and visions of great Americans—the poets and the seers." Ironically, Miller was just one of those people who wanted America to be great again, an America that refused to be seduced by "a false progress, a progress which stinks . . . [or] a world cluttered with useless objects which men and women, in order to be exploited and degraded, are taught to regard as useful. The dreamer whose dreams are non-utilitarian has no place in this world. Whatever does not lend itself to being bought and sold, whether in the realm of things, ideas, principles, dreams or hopes, is debarred."[14] It is a pity that the American patriot of the 1940s, and indeed, having seen all that has gone wrong since then, the patriot of today, have been equally unable to prize this book at its true worth, because it, more than any other work published in its day, diagnoses everything that has damaged the spirit of America, as it charged onward into a Brave New World where the only visionary is the entrepreneur. There was a time, in the United States, when snake-oil salesmen were mocked, or run out of a town—now our money in their pockets makes them modern-day heroes. That Miller saw all this, and more, in the early 1940s, is astonishing; that he told the extent of America's loss of principle so accurately is commendable. But there is more to *The Air-Conditioned Nightmare* than jeremiad, more than just the first thirteen or so pages of thrilling vitriol.

Having noted Miller's concern, as a good anarchist, with careful and disciplined observation of the natural world, it is rewarding to come across those moments in *The Air-Conditioned Nightmare* where he encounters select individuals who still live close to nature. For example, during his stay at The Shadows, a luxuriantly wild estate in New Iberia, Louisiana, he discovers that rich borderland between cultivated garden land and wild bayou:

> In the transparent black waters of the bayous the indestructible cypress, symbol of death and

silence, stands knee-deep. The sky is everywhere, dominating everything. . . . Always the
live oak, the cypress, the chinaball tree; always
the swamp, the clearing, the jungle; cotton,
rice, sugar cane; thickets of bamboo, banana
trees, gum trees, magnolias, cucumber trees,
swamp myrtle, sassafras. A wild profusion of
flowers: camellias, azaleas, roses of all kinds,
salvias, the giant spider lily, the aspidistra,
jasmine, Michaelmas daisies; snakes, screech-
owls, raccoons; moons of frightening dimen-
sions, lurid, pregnant, heavy as mercury. And
like a leitmotif to the immensity of sky are the
tangled masses of Spanish moss, that peculiar
spawn of the south which is allied to the pine-
apple family. An epiphyte, rather than a para-
site, it lives an independent existence, sustain-
ing itself on air and moisture; it flourishes just
as triumphantly on a dead tree or a telegraph
wire as on the live oak. "None but the Chinese,"
says Weeks Hall, "can ever hope to paint this
moss. It has a baffling secret of line and mass
which has never been remotely approached."[15]

Miller goes on to note that people from the
north and Midwest "actually shudder when they
first come upon the giant bewhiskered live oaks,
they sense something dismal and forbidding
about them. But when one sees them in majestic,

stately rows . . . one must bow down before them in humble adoration for they are, if not the monarchs of the tree world, certainly the sages or the magi." This entire passage is extraordinary—as is the eerily erotic scene where, coming upon a group of statues of the Four Seasons in a heavy mist while out walking the gardens at night, Miller tells us he "leaned over impulsively and kissed the marble lips. It was a strange sensation. I went to each of them in turn and kissed their cold, chaste lips." The descriptions of The Shadows offer a startling reminder of how varied Miller's gifts as a writer could be. Few readers of the more popular works, say, would guess that he could be a master nature writer, when he felt the occasion demanded but, in The Shadows, as in several passages of *The Colossus of Maroussi*, we catch glimpses of the brilliant nature writer Miller might have become, had he chosen to pursue that path.

Later, as he drives westward—the road trip an increasing source of worrying hilarity as his car troubles get worse and his ability to deal with them evaporates altogether—Miller encounters a man named Olsen whom he immediately sizes up as a "Desert Rat." This man has been all over the Southwest, especially the Painted Desert, studying its geology, its fossils, the Indian remains, the wildlife. He is a kind of citizen scientist before his time, with a touch of seer for good measure, and Miller is enchanted, especially when Olsen lays into the reductive "scientists" he has encountered in the desert, patronizing men who dismiss his theories without a second thought: "I figure that when we get too close to the secret Nature has a way of getting rid of us. Of course, we're getting smarter and smarter every day, but we never get to the bottom of things, and we never will. . . . We think we know a lot, but we think in a rut. Book people ain't more intelligent than other folk. They just learn how to read things a certain way. Put them in a new situation and they lose their heads. They ain't flexible. They only know how to think the way they were taught. That ain't intelligent to my way of thinkin'."

It may be noticed that this man sounds a lot like Miller himself—"The people who live the longest are the people who live the simplest. Money won't save you. Money makes you worry and fret. It's good to be alone and be silent. To do your own thinking" and "If [America] really set out to do something for the world, *unselfishly*, I believe we could succeed. But I don't think we'll do that. . . . We're put to save our big business international trade, and that sort of thing"—but it would be a harsh critic who didn't enjoy Olsen's company even if Miller did invent him. On the other hand, this encounter, and our author's openness to the old Desert Rat's ideas, illustrates one of Miller's favorite maxims perfectly: "Usually what is taught in school must be unlearned. Life is the teacher."[16] This is the real power of *The Air-conditioned Nightmare*, it is a supreme example of a writer allowing life, whether it be the people he meets, the land itself, the weather, or plain old car trouble, to be his teacher. Along the way, Miller does not set out to learn anything, but no lesson is lost. The adept owns nothing, but has the use of everything—and everywhere he goes, he either learns, or unlearns, something—and if they would allow the book to speak to them, even those who do not appreciate Miller's critique of his homeland would recognize *The Air-Conditioned Nightmare* as the great precursor to the most rewarding of American travel books, from Tom Wolfe's *The Electric Kool-Aid Acid Test* to William Least Heat-Moon's *Blue Highways* to Timothy O'Grady's *Divine Magnetic Lands*—and even the Hunter S. Thompson of *Fear and Loathing in Las Vegas*.

The Time of the Assassins

This refusal to mature, as we view it, has a quality of pathetic grandeur. Mature into what? we can imagine him asking himself. Into a manhood which spells enslavement and emasculation? He had blossomed prodigiously but—to flower? To flower meant to expire in corruption. He elects to die in the bud. It is the supreme gesture of youth triumphant.

—Henry Miller, *The Time of the Assassins:*
A Study of Rimbaud

Les couleurs propres de la vie se foncent, dansent, et se dégagent autour de la Vision, sur le chantier.[1]

—Arthur Rimbaud, *Illuminations*

The first thing to remember about Rimbaud, as a poet, is that he remains a boy for as long as he is actively writing. It is only when he leaves poetry that he becomes a man. In other words, he is not Baudelaire. One of the main attractions, for writers, is the unfinished quality of Rimbaud: like Heraclitus, like Sappho, like any other writer who leaves us what are, in a sense, fragments of a larger body of thought, this boy poet gifts us new spaces to play in—not just for interpretation, but also for expansions, elaborations, elucidations, justifications, and the armchair rebel's tacit agreement that what cannot be spoken of should remain beautifully unsaid. Yet while it is part of the writer's task to leave certain things untold (because he or she must trust, at times, to the reader's imagination), it is never his or her task simply to lapse into silence. Baudelaire understood this.[2] The difference between Rimbaud and Baudelaire (or, for that matter, Rimbaud and Thoreau) is that Rimbaud took the first step necessary for self-transformation—la *fuite*, the *dérèglement de tous les sens*, the sojourn in "Nature" in which the solitary spirit disconnects itself from the societal yoke—but he did not move on to the next step—or rather, he did not do so *on paper*. As Henry Miller notes, "[T]he only law which is really lived up to wholeheartedly and with a vengeance is the law of conformity. No wonder that as a mere lad [Rimbaud] ended 'by finding the disorder of his mind sacred.' At this point he had really made himself a seer. . . . Why could he not have compromised? Because compromise was not in his vocabulary. He was a fanatic from childhood, a person who had to go the whole hog or die. In this lies his purity, his innocence."[3] That may be. But what Rimbaud failed to recognize—understandably, given his youth, his social background, and his times—was that the compromise, for the writer who continues to work beyond the *voyant* stage of his development, is not with society, but with himself.

"No one can flatter himself that he is immune to the spirit of his own epoch," says Jung, "or even that he possesses a full understanding of it. Irrespective of our conscious convictions, each one of us, without exception, being a particle of the general mass, is somewhere attached to, coloured by, or even undermined by the spirit which goes through the mass. Freedom stretches only as far as the limits of our consciousness."[4] The problem of giving up the artist's—the anarchist's—vocation at the *voyant* stage, before the long discipline of coming to terms with what one has seen, is that the bad influence of societal conditioning (especially through the internalized figures of the parents against whom the seer rebels) lasts so very long. For the child, no matter how well he rebels against the more obvious elements of his conditioning, the stark gap in the emotional and sexual lives of his internalized parents, that pervasive and shaming disequilibrium, continues well into adulthood. Sometimes it is replicated, sometimes it is so fiercely rejected that there is nothing left to hold on to and work with. It may be, for many of us at least, that we never break free—or not fully. The sin of the parents is to demand that the child continue their lives for them.

It is, of course, unfair to compare Rimbaud with Baudelaire. We can never know what the former would have done, had he continued writing (interestingly, and rather amusingly, Miller compares Rimbaud to himself, saying that, in Rimbaud's story, "I rediscover my own plight. I have never relinquished the struggle. But what a price I have paid!"). As always, Miller is the hero of any story he tells—and in many ways, Rimbaud (to whose work he was introduced by his young rebel friends, John Dudley and Lafe Young of *The Air-Conditioned Nightmare*), or at least, the Rimbaud who appears in *The Time of the Assassins*, is as much a romantic alter-ego for Miller as he has been for thousands of self-styled poet-rebels who have taken to the road, and the pipe, in pursuit of the seer's life. For it is true now, and will remain so, that Rimbaud's initial predicament is shared by any intelligent child growing up in a society whose main purpose is to prepare its young people for a life of work and being adequately governed. Henri Laborit is right when he says that the socialization process aims at controlling every aspect of our lives, from the way we walk, to our sexual preferences, to how we think, and even to how and what we imagine.

Initially, this process is left in the hands of the education system, though the etymology of that term, *e-ducere* (to lead out, to bring out an individual's own gifts and abilities), is hardly commensurate with what actually happens in schools, youth groups, and the inevitable remedial centers that spring up to deal with the maladjusted and the maverick. Many a child who survives an industrial society's education system may remember the one teacher who saw some spark of possibility in that child's mind, a nub of stubborn creativity, a wisp of spirit, a hint of the true wild—but what that one exception does, all too often, is to prove the rule that, for the most part, the education system exists to impose approved societal standards, expectations, and limits more or less uniformly (though much depends on class and privilege, and occasionally luck). So, while it may seem cruel, and insufficiently appreciative of Rimbaud's youthful achievements in poetry, I want to suggest here that Rimbaud is, overall, a perfect model of the youthful rebel who defies the system that would control him, sometimes with real elegance, real grace, but who eventually falls away, defeated, exhausted, lost. Thus, while Miller stands alongside Rimbaud as the hero of *The Time of the Assassins*, he is also his most perceptive—and kindly—critic. Speaking of both Rimbaud and D. H. Lawrence as alter-egos in their fight against "the mothers," Miller makes the central point in any assessment of the rebel writer's work:

> All the rebelliousness which I share with them derives from this problem which, as nearly as I can express it, means the search to find one's true link with humanity. One finds it neither in the personal life nor in the collective life, if one is of this type. One is unadaptable to the point of madness. One longs to find his peer, but one is surrounded by vast empty spaces. One needs a teacher, but one lacks the humility, the flexibility, the patience which is demanded. One is not even at home or at ease with the great in spirit; even the highest are defective or suspect. And yet one has affinities only with these highest types. It is a dilemma fraught with the highest significance. One had to establish the ultimate difference of his own peculiar being and doing so discover his kinship with all humanity, even the very lowest. Acceptance is the key word. But acceptance is precisely the great stumbling block. It has to be total acceptance and not conformity.

Miller then goes on to say, just a page later:

> Rimbaud stressed the fact that he wanted liberty in salvation. But one is saved only by

surrendering this illusory freedom. The liberty he demanded was freedom for his ego to assert itself unrestrained. That is not freedom. Under this illusion one can, if one lives long enough, play out every facet of one's being and still find cause to complain, ground to rebel. It is a kind of liberty which grants one the right to object, to secede if necessary. It does not take into account other people's differences, only one's own. It will never aid one to find one's link, one's communion, with all mankind. One remains forever separate, forever isolate.[5]

Miller goes on to compare Rimbaud to Van Gogh, but I feel, still, that it would have been more rewarding to bring in Baudelaire here—for one of Baudelaire's great achievements as an artist is to go beyond the desire for an illusory freedom of the ego, in order to accept himself as he is, in a communal, if oppositional, context and so find a *historical* link with all humankind. Baudelaire finds it in himself to object, but not to secede: by a supreme act of artistic discipline he came to a place where, standing alone, he nevertheless enters into a brotherhood of men that, in Miller's words, "consists not in thinking alike, nor in acting alike, but in aspiring to praise creation. The song of creation springs from the ruins of earthly endeavor. The outer man dies away in order to reveal the golden bird which is winging its way towards divinity."[6] Though I am not sure I would, myself, stand by all of the language here (I would probably prefer an ordinary skylark, or a regular flamingo, to some firebird of myth) I do believe that, among the French poets, Baudelaire, and elsewhere, Rilke, or Montale (to name two Europeans more or less at random) were exemplars of a poetic discipline that, having passed through the necessary stage of *être un voyant*, returns to the common light of day with new vision and no particular need for the wings of angels.[7]

So why is it that Rimbaud is such an important figure for the rebel artist? Why does Miller choose to write an entire book—often incisive, sometimes repetitive, occasionally a little too busy with its own rhetoric—on this boy, rather than, say, the grown-man, Baudelaire? I think much of Rimbaud's vogue, especially among the young, has to do with our retrospective knowledge of what was waiting to emerge from the European darkness. In the post-Auschwitz, post-Nagasaki, post-natural world we now inhabit, it can seem, at least by day, that all *place* is lost—that the living places of Being Beauteous, where life's very own colors darken and dance and shift around the emerging Vision, are so few and far between that they have become mere curiosities. Perhaps they always were to industrial, "bourgeois" society. Paradoxically, however, the more depleted the life of the day has become, the richer the dusk has begun to seem, so that the night seems to be full of a truly pagan beauty and grace that must conceal itself in the darkness to survive the overall degradation of the developed world (and this, it seems to me, is key: this idea of *the pagan*, the life of the land, the nature, to paraphrase Rilke, with which we fall into harmony by *choosing* it). In that depleted world, it can seem that all real life has taken to the shadows, to the corners, to subways and cellar bars and underground tunnels, to the drug den, the freak show, the dark end of the fair, as the only venues where it may reveal its tainted beauty—a beauty that is both forbidden and accursed. This is the source of modernist nostalgia: this dusk. It would seem wonderfully ironic, then, that the rebel who passes through the search for "freedom" and emerges renewed into the common light of day may well arrive at another kind of nostalgia altogether, the nostalgia that informs the work of those writers who, in the twentieth century, really did illuminate our shared creaturely world—a nostalgia for the mysteries of a Wednesday afternoon, when tea is warmer than absinthe, and a stray wisp of smoke from the stove is more intoxicating than "le rêve d'un hachischin." Is Miller one of that band of illuminators? It would be wonderful, given his image, to be able to say that he is—and in many ways, his best works, *The Time of the Assassins* included, would go a long way toward justifying that claim.

The Creature World

> Out yonder they may curse, revile, and torture
> one another, defile all the human instincts, make
> a shambles of creation (if it were in their power),
> but here, no, here, it is unthinkable, here there is
> abiding peace, the peace of God, and the serene
> security created by a handful of good neighbors
> living at one with the creature world.
>
> —Henry Miller, *Big Sur and the Oranges
> of Hieronymus Bosch*

> Quand je m'y suis mis quelquefois à considérer
> les diverses agitations des hommes et les périls
> et les peines où ils s'exposent, dans la cour, dans
> la guerre, d'où naissent tant de querelles, de pas-
> sions, d'entreprises hardies et souvent mauvaises,
> etc. j'ai dit souvent que tout le malheur des hom-
> mes vient d'une seule chose, qui est de ne savoir
> plus demeurer en repos dans une chambre.[1]
>
> —Blaise Pascal, *Pensées*

When we consider much of what Henry Miller
wrote and said about worldly success, it may
come as a surprise to know that, during the last
few years of his life, he actively campaigned to
win the Nobel Prize. In 1978, he even sent out

one of his famous round-robin letters, asking, not for money (as he often did: even when the books were selling and film rights were being bought up, Miller never had any cash; he was always giving it away) but for help in influencing the Academy: "Dear Friend," he wrote, to a number of friends (including, with an irony nobody could invent, the man who would go on to win the Nobel that year, Isaac Bashevis Singer), "In my attempt to obtain the Nobel Prize for Literature this coming year I hope to enlist your support. All I ask is for you to write a few succinct lines to: Nobel Committee of the Swedish Academy, Borshuset, 11129 Stockholm, Sweden. Please note that the committee urgently requests that the name of the proposed candidate not be publicized. Sincerely, Henry Miller." Later, when he heard that Singer had won, he quickly revised his plan, assuring the very same friends to whom he had just written that his plan had always been to mount the campaign in 1979. Once again, those unfortunate correspondents duly wrote in, but the prize went to the Greek poet Odysseus Elytis, cited by the Swedish Academy "for his poetry, which, against the background of Greek tradition, depicts with sensuous strength and intellectual clear-sightedness modern man's struggle for freedom and creativeness."[2] Ironically, it would be hard to find a more apt summation of

Miller's work. What was both revealing and galling, however, was the remark made by a member of the Academy to Lawrence Durrell, to the effect that the judges were waiting for Miller "to become respectable."[3]

It seems odd, and a little unsettling, to think of Miller pursuing this corrupt world's honors so devotedly. However, he had always fantasized about the Nobel Prize and, according to his friend Brassaï, had started talking about the possibility during the late 1950s.[4] To some readers, this has made Miller seem less admirable—less independent, less unworldly—but what they perhaps fail to appreciate is just how hard it is, for the literary writer, to live with the constant suspicion of inevitable failure that comes with the job. For one thing, over a lifetime of labor, the financial rewards are comparatively meager. (Miller said he wanted the Nobel, not for the glory, but for the money, so he could pay off his taxes.) Considering his socialization—and it's not that much different now, truth be told—it comes as no surprise that Miller always felt a nagging doubt about himself as a writer and as a man.[5] For much of his life, the books that would make his reputation were banned; when they did emerge, they were subjected to a flurry of criticism that, while justified in some ways, did miss the central point of what he was trying to do. His experimental techniques with the novel were often adopted by others, who made such compromises as allowed them to achieve both sales and critical respect. As with so many artistic pioneers, Miller was too much, too difficult, too confrontational and, at times, "too dark" for a wider audience—which meant that, the further he went, the deeper he dug, the more risks he took, the less successful, in paying-the-rent terms, he was doomed to be.

A friend of mine calls this The Cassandra Dilemma: do the work well, push the bounds, honestly, and with rigor, and the closer you are to getting it right can be measured fairly accurately by how much attention "the world" takes. You can go *so* far, but no further. (This, it has to be said, is more true now than it ever has been, but today the bugbears are darkness, intensity, and honest complexity, rather than shock value or supposed obscenity. Nothing is verboten; it just has to come as a sound bite.) The mainstream reader knows what he wants, and that is entertainment with a veneer of "the real," the challenge of a problem that he can solve, a soupçon of flattery, and a dollop of sex (just as long as it's *grey*). What such a reader doesn't want is an invitation to change his life, or a clear exposition of how rotten the system is, à la Henry Miller, because, as my friend says, that is *depressing*. To write outside the mainstream, to diagnose the system's ills, to lay your heart and your spirit out on the page, is lonely work, but it feels lonelier still to think that you did it all for nothing.

So it shouldn't be surprising that Miller coveted the Nobel—even with his tongue in his cheek. Nor should it surprise us that, at the same time, he understood perfectly well that worldly success wasn't just an illusion, but was also dangerous to the writer. In a little chapbook he put out at the very end of his life, he had this to say on the matter: "If you have had a successful career, as presumably I have had, the late years may not be the happiest time of your life. (Unless you've learned to swallow your own shit.) Success, from the worldly standpoint, is like the plague for a writer who still has something to say. Now, when he should be enjoying a little leisure, he finds himself more occupied than ever. Now he is the victim of his fans and well wishers, of all those who desire to exploit his name. Now it is a different kind of struggle that one has to wage. The problem now is how to keep free, how to do only what one wants to do"—adding that what mattered was to retain a sense of curiosity, and wonder: "With this attribute goes another which I prize above everything else, and that is the sense of wonder. No matter how restricted my world may become I cannot imagine it leaving me void of wonder. In a sense I suppose it might be called my religion. I do not ask how it came about, this creation in which we swim, but only to enjoy and appreciate it."[6]

There is an obvious cognitive dissonance here—there always is. Prizes, sales, prestige (though not celebrity) are alluring. Besides, to win a prestigious prize is not only to obtain the wherewithal to cancel those worrying tax bills (or pay the grocery bill, or the children's college fees), it is also to add weight to what one considers a greater good. Miller's friend, Seferis, accepting the Nobel in 1972, chose to see the award as a mark of the Academy's esteem for Greek poetic *tradition* that "is characterized by love of the human; justice is its norm. In the tightly organized classical tragedies the man who exceeds his measure is punished by the Erinyes. And this norm of justice holds even in the realm of nature." No doubt, had Miller won the prize in 1980 (which was rumored to be "his year," until he died too soon to be considered; in the event, the prize went to Czeslaw Milosz), he would have spoken of wonder, of acceptance, and, perhaps, of "the creature world," a vision that had begun to form during his sojourn in Greece and had gradually developed, not into an organized system of thought (something we can hardly expect from Miller), but into a profound earthly vision that foreshadows even the most recent work in philosophical ecology and emerging ideas around "the creaturely" and biotic interanimation. That vision has been given other names. For a time, I think, Rimbaud meant the same thing when he spoke of Being Beauteous.[7] James P. Carse has called it "the infinite game," seeing the entire sphere of being as a game that encompasses all other (i.e., finite) games, investing them with value while setting them in a context that, while it does not diminish anything, nevertheless reveals their transitory nature: "There are at least two kinds of games," Carse says. "One could be called finite, the other, infinite. A finite game is played for the purpose of winning, an infinite game for the purpose of continuing the play," adding that "[h]uman freedom is not a freedom over nature; it is the freedom to be natural, that is, to answer to the spontaneity of nature with our own spontaneity. Though we are free to be natural, we are not free by nature; we are free by culture, by history." And he concludes, "It is not necessary for infinite players to be Christians; indeed, it is not possible for them to be Christians—seriously. Neither is it possible for them to be Buddhists, or Muslims, or atheists, or New Yorkers—seriously. All such titles can only be playful abstractions, mere performances for the sake of laughter. Infinite players are not serious actors in any story, but the joyful poets of a story that continues to originate what they cannot finish. . . . There is but one infinite game."[8]

It should have taken a couple of hours, but it ended up being a day-long schlepp comprising three tedious hops, first, after an hour's delay, from Grenada to Madrid, then a long wait at Madrid for the next flight, and then, after yet another long delay, from Birmingham to Edinburgh. I have no memory of why all this happened; all I remember now is that, on that last flight, I died for a while, just as the plane was coming in to land. This is not proven scientific fact (I managed to escape the paramedics when I came to), but it *was* my experience: I was sitting in my seat, 1A, by the window, looking out over the familiar hills, when suddenly my entire body ceased to be, and I ascended—just a little—into a pure whiteness, though not the ever-afterish white light common to stories of this kind (don't worry, I am not about to claim that Jesus or my favorite uncle came to meet me in the afterworld, and there will, most assuredly, be no angels in this account). No: it wasn't a light; it was more a kind of blankness. Like the space in a Chinese painting of mist or fog, say, or the untouched white paper in Karl Schmidt-Rottluff's woodcut from 1905, *Bäume im Winter*, that I once saw at the Brücke Museum, Berlin, a whiteness that suggests both snow and the nothingness that haunts being. This whiteness *was*, in fact, a nothingness, but it was also active—I have difficulty, explaining this, without resorting to the classics, in this case, the *Hagakure* of Tsunetomo Yamamoto: "Our bodies are given form from the midst of nothingness. Existing where there is nothing is the meaning of the phrase 'Form is emptiness.' That all things are provided for by nothingness is the meaning of the phrase, 'Emptiness is form.' One should not think that these are two separate"[9]—and I knew that its action upon me (my body and my person, as well as my soul, or spirit) was to dissolve it utterly. Not to destroy it, as such, but to break it down to the most basic state, the way a leaf, fallen from the tree in October, becomes sweet liquor in the soil, for other plants to feed on come springtime. Though I feel I must add, here, that I don't mean this altogether literally. If I have to use one word for what I anticipated, at that moment—which I did, quite honestly, think would be my last—I would say that, in that white space, I expected to be absolved, or perhaps, *acquitted* of presence. However, like those more familiar stories of near-death experiences, my exit didn't quite come about, and, some time later—it must have been a fair amount of time, because the plane was now on the ground and most of the passengers had departed—I found myself gazing up into the face of a woman who looked some-what familiar.

It would be satisfying to report more about my imaginary near-death experience, but the truth is that, after the whiteness everything else was pure anticlimax, bordering on farce. I had "re-gained consciousness" (that really *isn't* the right term) in the yellowish glow you might find in a snow globe, expecting more than the two flight attendants who were working on me, one loos-ening an already loose collar, the other speaking, asking me if I knew my name, or maybe saying my name, it wasn't entirely clear. It all felt pain-fully intimate: the attendant who was speaking seemed to be looking into my face from inches away and, at the same time, she also seemed im-possibly distant, almost fictional, like a movie ghost, or an apparition. I think, for a moment, I had really believed I was about to enter that cli-chéd next-life scenario I had read about—mostly in doctors' waiting rooms, where the magazines seem, one would have thought inappropriately, to specialize in such matters—and I imagine that I had been hoping for a long-dead girlfriend to have turned up by now—the girl I once fell for when I worked in a food processing factory, say, a girl who went home one evening and died un-expectedly in her sleep, come, now, to guide me into the light, or perhaps to some other cliché.

But as it turns out, I hadn't died in seat 1A after all, I'd just passed out rather forcefully, and this was not the afterlife, it was just *after*. And I can see, now, that we were all disappointed: the younger of the flight attendants in particular, who was a little too insistent in her refusal to believe me when I assured her I was fine (clearly, I wasn't, and I felt decidedly out of sorts for the next several minutes) and that I was ready to go on alone. It seems that the paramedics had already been summoned and were waiting in the terminal (how long *had* I been unconscious?) and the young woman, pretty even by flight attendant standards, with reddish-blonde hair tied back in a tight ponytail and very blue eyes, seemed to think I was spoiling something by not playing my designated role. For a moment, I was even tempted to capitulate and allow myself to be guided away, but I have a horror of hospitals and, besides, I wanted to get home, after a long absence. So I insisted I would be fine and walked away on my own two feet, and though I felt ill for days after, I managed to pass the whole incident off as a more than usual degree of travel fatigue.

Nevertheless, that whiteness stayed in my mind, a visible nothingness, and I felt oddly grateful for it—I still do—and for the premonition I'd been vouchsafed of the emptiness that, for now, gives my body form. For a moment, I had known, in Henry Miller's words, "what the great cure is: it is to give up, to relinquish, to surrender, so that our little hearts may beat in unison with the great heart of the world."[10] More important, I could think those words again without dismissing them because I was embarrassed by their raw emotion, or what my dutiful British mind was trained to reject as "sentimental." For now, I had been treated to a live demonstration of something that, till then, I had only known as a word. I had been given, in real, experiential terms the understanding that I was not merely human, but creaturely. "Once I thought that to be human was the highest aim a man could have, but I see now that it was meant to destroy me. To-day I am proud to say that I am inhuman, that I belong not to men and governments, that I have nothing to do with creeds and principles. I have nothing to do with the creaking machinery of humanity—I belong to the earth!"[11]

So says Miller in *Tropic of Cancer*—and at one time, certainly in my mid-twenties, I thought this was mostly bravado. I had put in my years as sub–Rimbaud wanderer—I had slept on gravestones in old city churchyards and sat in city parks with my hashish-filled corncob pipe, watching children play tag; I had written poems and thrown them away; every year, I gave away any property I had amassed, other than a few books and some clothes; I had worked in the kitchens and gardens and sewers of "The System"—and, to date, I had learned only one thing: that men and governments are *everywhere*. I had pledged to do nothing that would support the system I loathed, but that didn't mean that it did not govern my life. For one thing, it had power over my body in at least one sense: it could either prohibit my consumption of hashish and LSD, or, if I chose to continue to practice what I thought of as my "sacrament," it could throw me in jail for seven years. In those days, as I recall, this was a major concern for people in my walk of life. We were drop-outs, refuseniks, *étrangers*—but I couldn't really kid myself: I was powerless, as myself, and even if I wasn't contributing to the system in a meaningful way (making money, taking orders, voting etcetera etcetera), I still had to labor in its poisoned vineyards to obtain my daily bread. That I was also breaking its laws was not much consolation, when I knew that, should it come to it, I wouldn't last a day in prison.

Then, slowly, as I mowed the lawns and dredged the ornamental pond in my last garden job—slowly, quietly, as befits a revelation in a garden, I began to understand the key point: belonging. Yes, Miller was like any other man who lived in the civilized world: he had to endure men and governments, creeds and principles, but he did not *belong* to them. On the other hand, he could choose to belong to the earth—even while that earth was being hopelessly poisoned by men and governments and the profit principle. For belonging *is* a choice. At that point, I was reading Robinson Jeffers, poems like "Roan Stallion":

> Humanity is
> the start of the race; I say
> Humanity is the mould to break away from,
>   the crust to break

and I had thrilled at the closing lines of "Carmel Point":

> As for us:
> We must uncenter our minds from ourselves;
> We must unhumanize our views a little, and
>   become confident
> As the rock and ocean that we were made
>   from.[12]

I did not see any of this as an expression of spite, or even anger with the enemy; for me, it was the necessary recognition of a rift between self and the societal world, not just as a refusal to take part in the race (a refusal that granted me a kind of boho status that, in James Carse's terms, could only be seen as a kind of title, or badge of honor) but a departure point from which to imagine an alternative. The first step—a considered *Non serviam*—was incomplete without the second—*être un voyant*—but then, after the *dérèglement*, after the years in the desert, or on the road, or at Walden Pond, the final step was to become new, by choosing to belong, not to the tribe, or the society, but to the earth and to what Miller, in spite of his occasional posturing, still called "the great heart of the world." Is it a contradiction to want to become "inhuman" and at the same time, wish for one's heart to beat in unison with all of the rest of creation, including other humans? I do not think so; instead, I think it is the definition of what Miller means by "the creature world" and what we mean by "creaturely": what Miller saw was that we needed to abandon the limits imposed by civilization and discover anew the spontaneous, hazardous, beauteous being that might allow us to belong to the earth, without wishing to appropriate or control it.

In his novel, *Zero K*, Don DeLillo describes the sojourn of a man named Jeffrey Lockhart at a remote cryogenics facility where his stepmother, currently suffering from the early stages of a terminal illness, is waiting to undergo a procedure that will freeze her body until it can be repaired, sometime in the future. The facility is called The Convergence, and, as Jeffrey explores it and encounters its denizens, it becomes clear that those involved in its foundation and business are visionaries, men and women who are working for a new language, new meanings, new and unimaginable systems. One of those visionaries, a man named Ben-Ezra[13] (who is discovered in a "proper English Garden" in which everything, even the plants, is artificial), proposes an experiment to Jeffrey:

> You sit alone in a quiet room at home and you listen carefully. What is it you hear? Not traffic in the street, not voices or rain or someone's radio. . . . You hear something but what? It's not room tone or ambient sound. It's something that may change as your listening deepens, second after second, and the sound is growing louder now—not louder but somehow wider, sustaining itself, encircling you. What Is it? The mind, the life itself, your life? Or is it the world, not the material mass, land and sea, but what inhabits the world, the flood of human existence. The world hum. Do you hear it, yourself, ever?[14]

It is a profoundly beautiful and troubling vision: the world hum, the hum of all human existence, carrying on, everywhere. Unstoppable. Is it possible to think of that hum and not be almost overwhelmed by a sense, on the one hand, of its sheer vulnerability—a vulnerability occasioned by its own massive and all-consuming presence in a world of finite resources—and, on the other, of its immense beauty? It is this hum that, more likely than not, will end the world as we know it. It is this mass of humanity that will consume our world, just as a flock of locusts consumes a field of grain. And yet it is to this hum that we most surely belong. Having heard it, we cannot deny it. Indeed, how possible is it not to love that eerie music, which is *us*?

In a 2015 interview, Lawrence Ferlinghetti remarked, in relation to angry responses to his poem "Overpopulation": "Probably the one problem behind all the other crises on earth right now is overpopulation. You could take any daily newspaper and probably 60% of the stories could be traced back to some overpopulation cause. For instance, why do loggers want to cut down rain forests? Because people need more houses. Why do they need more houses? Because there's a huge increase in population worldwide."[15] Ferlinghetti is not alone. For many in the developed world, any concern with rising population figures is perceived a sign of inherent fascism, or racism, or sexism, or a combination of all three. Those concerned with population are said to be intent on controlling the lives and breeding rights of others. But the truth remains that the land—the soil, the sea, the other creatures with whom we share this planet—cannot meaningfully survive the current exponential growth in human population. If we continue as we are, we are doomed. Even if the human population could carry on for a while longer, the stress on the forests, seas, air, soil, and climate of the planet would lead to a way of life that many of us could not tolerate.[16] At the same time, there is nothing we can think of, at present, to halt our journey toward, if not extinction, then at least massive breakdown. Like the children in *Jude the Obscure*, "we are too menny." On the other hand, we cannot deny others the right to have children, and we cannot refuse them the "right" to own and use the consumer goods and services that we take for granted. And why would we? They, like us, are part of the hum. They are our *kind*.

Later, back at The Convergence, Jeffrey tries to repeat Ben-Ezra's experiment: "I went to my room, turned on the light and sat in the chair thinking. It felt as though I'd done this a thousand times, same room every time, same person in the chair. I found myself listening. I tried to empty my mind and simply listen. I wanted to hear what Ben-Ezra had described, the oceanic sound of people living and thinking and talking, billions, everywhere, waiting for trains, marching to war, licking food off their fingers. Or simply being who they were. The world hum."[17]

This, then, is our tragedy. As a species, we have been too successful in certain areas, and miserable failures in others. Miller saw this clearly back in the 1940s:

> It is not enough to overthrow governments, masters, tyrants: one must overthrow his own preconceived ideas of right and wrong, good and bad, just and unjust. We must abandon the hard-fought trenches we have dug ourselves into and come out into the open, surrender our arms, our possessions, our rights as individuals, classes, nations, peoples. A billion men seeking peace cannot be enslaved. We have enslaved ourselves, by our own petty, circumscribed view of life. It is glorious to offer one's life for a cause, but dead men accomplish nothing. Life demands that we offer something more— spirit, soul, intelligence, goodwill. Nature is ever ready to repair the gaps caused by death, but nature cannot supply the intelligence, the will, the imagination to conquer the forces of death. Nature restores and repairs, that is all. It is man's task to eradicate the homicidal instinct which is infinite in its ramifications and manifestations. It is useless to call upon God, as it is futile to meet force with force."[18]

Does Miller frame his argument in such terms because he knows it is too radical, in the current climate? Almost certainly. However, as true anarchists everywhere know, the collapse toward which we are headed can only be avoided by making the sacrifices Miller describes—and if we do not give up those illusions of power and ownership, they will, in due course, be taken from us.

"To keep the mind empty is a feat, a very healthful feat too," Miller says, elsewhere in *The Colossus of Maroussi*.

> To be silent the whole day long, see no newspaper, hear no radio, listen to no gossip, be thoroughly and completely lazy, thoroughly and completely indifferent to the fate of the world is the finest medicine a man can give himself. The book-learning gradually dribbles away; problems melt and dissolve; ties are gently severed; thinking, when you deign to indulge in it, becomes very primitive; the body becomes a new and wonderful instrument; you look at plants or stones or fish with different eyes; you wonder what people are struggling to accomplish by their frenzied activities; you know there is a war on but you haven't the faintest idea what it's about or why people should enjoy killing one another.[19]

What I have been seeking in this chapter might sound like a slightly crazed eco-critical reading of Miller's thought; I believe it is not. In fact, it is, for me, more pressing and personal than that. I have said that I did not go back to Miller to write lit-crit; I wanted to find work that would provoke me to think anew about what I take for granted, whether it be with regard to the writer's vocation and social function (if there is one), the battle lines drawn up between the sexes by a society that remains sexually and sensually repressive, or the idea of the creaturely in philo-sophical and ecological terms. In this closing sec-tion, what I want is to use Miller's ideas as much to critique *mainstream* ecology/environmental methods as to attack The System itself—because, as Miller's work and life show, there can be no compromise with The System, no matter how green or democratic it pretends to be. Business is business and as long as the world is driven by profit, titles, and power relations, we must look to those who propose radical acts, in our flights, and in our discoveries—and the basis of that radical vision is the sense of "creatureliness" that informs anarchist thinking.

Again, this already sounds too highfalutin and solemn: another way of describing my in-tention throughout might be to say that I have been trying to recover and reimagine a seriously playful condition ("here all is play and inven-tion") in which "the world has not to be put in order: the world is order incarnate. It is for us to put ourselves in unison with this order," or in James Carse's terms, to become infinite players. Too many self-described eco-critical writers are prepared to compromise with power for finite titles, short-term achievements (the most base of which is surely "power-sharing"), or even just a few drops of hope in a parched land; too many environmentalists find themselves able to back corporations and landowners whose greenwashing is sufficiently persuasive; too many green politicians are prepared to put the world in order if it means "keeping the lights on"; and, sadly, we are very far from reaching the stage 'where the environment (the earth, natural order, the hum of all living things) is the main concern in all— *all*—of our decisions. Does it sound too radical, really, to say that the lights have to go off now and then? Does it really seem misanthropic to suggest that the earth cannot sustain a population of nine billion, if that population still sees it as a right to keep their lights on (and their cars on the road, and the air-con running day and night)? Miller knew what was stake, and there are times when his writing justifiably hints at apocalypse, or at the very least, the massive ruination of a "developed society" that didn't, in the end, deserve to continue. It would be wrong not to allow him the last word here—but, because his view of the world is so manifold, because, like his hero, Whitman, he contradicts himself in order to add to the joy and the confusion, I offer two remarks to keep in mind as we stumble on into the darkness, or the (natural) light:

> When God answers Job cosmologically it is to remind man that he is only a part of creation, that it is his duty to put himself in accord with it or perish. When man puts his head out of the stream of life he becomes self-conscious. And with self-consciousness comes arrest, fixation, symbolised so vividly by the myth of Narcissus.[20]

and

> The universe is run by laws, if you break the law you have to pay the penalty. That's only fair, isn't it? Besides, how are you going to learn except through experience?[21]

⬢ NOTES

BY WAY OF A PREFACE

1. Kate Millett, *Sexual Politics* (Garden City, NY: Doubleday, 1970).

2. Henry Miller, "An Open Letter to Surrealists Everywhere," in *The Cosmological Eye* (New York: New Directions, 1939).

3. "Je dis qu'il faut être voyant, se faire voyant. Le poète se fait voyant par un long, immense et raisonné dérèglement de tous les sens." Arthur Rimbaud, letter to Paul Demeny, May 15, 1871, in Rimbaud, *Poésies, Une saison en enfer, Illuminations*, ed. Louis Forestier (Paris: Gallimard, 1973).

4. Jeannette Winterson, "The Male Mystique of Henry Miller," *New York Times*, January 26, 2012.

5. In this Miller reminds us of Frank Harris and other sexual "adventurers" of the Victorian and Edwardian eras, of whom more later. Because the "sex" being discussed in these works is mostly a matter of conquest, the exercise of power and revenge against a puritanical society, it is hardly surprising that love plays no part in these tales. Henry Miller, interview by

Terry Gifford, "Dirty Old Henry Miller at 86," *Chicago Tribune*, February 1978.

6. Tokuda quoted in R. J. Hudson, "Letters by Henry Miller to Hoki Tokuda Miller," September 27, 2006, LiveJournal, https://community.livejournal.com/--henrymiller/3939.html.

7. Letter from Miller to Tokuda, 1966, quoted in ibid.

8. This culture, referred to universally by sexual adventurers and bohemians as "puritan," not only deprived women of self-expression and sexual freedom but, by the same token, forced sexually active men into a kind of trickster role, intent on "stealing" from the puritan world the freedoms that might otherwise have been a matter of negotiation and mutual agreement.

9. Thus, in a real sense, we can see that Hoki, as a person, is irrelevant to the *mono no aware* process. She could be anyone.

10. Walter Raleigh, "The Silent Lover," in *The Poems of Sir Walter Raleigh*, ed. John Hannah (London: George Bell and Sons, 1892).

11. Marianne Moore, "Poetry," in *New Collected Poems of Marianne Moore*, ed. Heather Cass White (London: Faber, 2017).

12. "Surely everyone realizes, at some point along the way, that he is capable of living a far better life than the one he has chosen." Henry Miller, *On Turning Eighty*, Capra Chapbook series, no. 1 (Santa Barbara, CA: Capra Press, 1972).

13. Henry Miller, *The Time of the Assassins* (New York: New Directions, 1962), 5.

14. Johann Wolfgang von Goethe, "The Experiment as Mediator of Object and Subject" (1792), trans. Craig Holdrege, The Nature Institute, http://natureinstitute.org/pub/ic/ic24/ic24_goethe.pdf.

15. Hart Crane, "Chaplinesque," in *The Complete Poems and Selected Letters and Prose of Hart Crane*, ed. Brom Weber (New York: Liveright, 1966).

IN PRAISE OF FLIGHT

1. Henri Laborit, *Éloge de la fuite* (Paris: Editions Robert Laffont, 1976).

2. André Gide, *Les faux-monnayeurs* (Paris: Gallimard, 1925).

3. Henry Miller, interview by *People* magazine, August 21, 1978.

4. Henry Miller, *Tropic of Capricorn* (London: Penguin Modern Classics, 2015).

5. Terence, *Heauton Timorumenos*, ed. John Carew Rolfe (Charleston, SC: Nabu Press, 2010).

6. For example, *Éloge de la fuite*, an extraordinary work, remains untranslated, for the moment, though non-Francophone readers interested in knowing more about Laborit's philosophy should see Alain Resnais's 1980 film, *Mon oncle d'Amérique* (My American uncle) for a typically unconventional exploration of his ideas. His two works that have been translated are *Stress and Cellular Function* (Philadelphia: Lippincott, 1959); and *Decoding the Human Message* (London: Allison and Busby, 1977).

7. Largactil was marketed as Thorazine in the United States. It should not be forgotten, however, that chlorpromazine-like drugs have more recently been subject to significant abuses, especially in the off-label treatment of children and the elderly and as constituents of the so-called pharmacological lobotomy used to keep mental health patients docile.

8. *Éloge de la fuite*, Avant-propos (the rough translation of this passage, cited in French on the first page of this chapter, is my own).

9. Jonathan Meades describes this fundamental stage, somewhat differently, as "seeking shelter, food, sex and narcosis." Jonathan Meades, *Museums without Walls* (London: Unbound, 2013).

10. Laborit, *Éloge de la fuite*.

11. Henry Miller, *Tropic of Cancer*, new ed. (London: Harper Perennial, 2005).

12. George Dibbern, *Quest* (New York: W. W. Norton, 1941).

13. Letter from Miller to Dibbern, April 17, 1945, quoted in Erika Grundmann, *Dark Sun: Te Rapunga and the Quest of George Dibbern* (Northland, NZ: David Ling Publishing, 2004), http://georgedibbern.com/DarkSun/DS-Chapter.html.

14. All information on Dibbern comes from George Dibbern's Quest and Life (http://www.georgedibbern.com /aboutdibbern.html), a website dedicated to Dibbern's life and work, maintained by Erika Grundmann, author of the Dibbern biography *Dark Sun*.

15. Dibbern, *Quest*.

16. Henry Miller, *Tropic of Cancer*, new ed. (London: Harper Perennial, 2005).

17. Tsunetomo Yamamoto, *Hagakure: The Book of the Samurai* (Boulder, CO: Shambhala Publications, 2012).

18. The review of *Quest*, by George Dibbern, is collected in Henry Miller, *Stand Still Like the Hummingbird* (New York: New Directions, 1962).

LIKE A FLUID (THE FALSE PORNOGRAPHER)

1. Henri Laborit, *Éloge de la fuite* (Paris: Editions Robert Laffont, 1976). "To love another is to accept that he or she is free to think, feel, and act in a way that does not conform to my wishes, or to my own gratification, to accept that he or she lives in accordance with his or her system of personal gratification and not in accordance with mine" (my translation).

2. See André Dubus, *Voices from the Moon* (Boston: David R Godine, 1984).

3. According to Harris, "There are two main traditions of English writing: the one of perfect liberty, that of Chaucer

and Shakespeare, completely outspoken, with a certain liking for lascivious details and witty smut, a man's speech: the other emasculated more and more by puritanism and since the French Revolution, gelded to tamest propriety; for that upheaval brought the illiterate middle-class to power and insured the domination of girl-readers. Under Victoria, English prose literature became half childish, as in stories of 'Little Mary' or at best provincial, as anyone may see who cares to compare the influence of Dickens, Thackeray and Reade in the world with the influence of Balzac, Flaubert and Zola." Frank Harris, *My Life and Loves* (New York: Grove Press, 1963). So it is that men like Harris even dictate, not only the kind of stories that may be told, but the tone and style of the telling.

4. Anon., *The Way of a Man with a Maid* (1908), in *The Wordsworth Book of Classic Erotica* (Ware: Wordsworth Editions, 2007).

5. Kate Millett, *Sexual Politics* (Garden City, NY: Doubleday, 1970), chap. 1.

6. Frank Harris, *My Life and Loves: Five Volumes in One/ Complete and Unexpurgated* (New York: Grove Press, 1963).

7. Miller learned this as much from D. H. Lawrence as from Harris and the other Georgian pornographers.

8. "While there may still be plenty of ads promoting a 'Quick and Easy Divorce for $299,' that price is usually for couples who have already agreed on the terms of their divorce and just need a lawyer to sign off. Bruce Cameron of Cameron Law PLLC in Rochester, Minn. says the generally accepted figure is anywhere from $15,000 to $20,000. 'Basically it costs as much to get unmarried as it does to get married,' says Cameron." Laura Seldon, "How Much Does the Average Divorce Really Cost?," *Huffington Post*, May 30, 2013, http://www.huffingtonpost.com/galtime/how-much-does-the-average_b_3360433.html.

9. Centers for Disease Control / National Center for Health Statistics, National Vital Statistics System. https://www.cdc.gov/nchs/nvss/marriage_divorce_tables.htm.

10. Meredith Dank et al., *Estimating the Size and Structure of the Underground Commercial Sex Economy in Eight Major US Cities*, Urban Institute, March 12, 2014, http://www.urban.org/research/publication/estimating-size-and-structure-underground-commercial-sex-economy-eight-major-us-cities.

11. Henry Miller, interview by *People* magazine, August 21, 1978.

12. Henry Miller, *Sexus* (London: Penguin Modern Classics, 2015).

13. Henry Miller, *The Time of the Assassins* (New York: New Directions, 1962), 12.

14. Henry Miller, *Sextet* (New York: New Directions, 2010).

ON LOVE AND PROPERTY

1. John Stoltenberg, *Refusing to Be a Man* (Portland, OR: Breitenbush Books, 1989).

2. Henry Miller, *Tropic of Capricorn* (London: Penguin Modern Classics, 2015).

3. Jack Achiezer Guggenheim, "The Evolution of Chutzpah as a Legal Term," *Kentucky Law Journal* 87, no. 2 (1998–99).

4. Jack Gilbert, *Collected Poems* (New York: Knopf, 2014).

5. Theodore Roosevelt, "Manhood and Statehood," address at the celebration of statehood, Colorado Springs, CO, August 2, 1901, Almanac of Theodore Roosevelt, http://www.theodore-roosevelt.com/images/research/txtspeeches/670.pdf.

HENRY MILLER AS ANARCHIST

1. "The same bourgeois magic / wherever the mail-train drops us off. / The most elementary physicist feels that it is no longer possible / to submit to this personal atmosphere, this

fog of physical remorse, / and that even to notice it is already an affliction" (my translation).

2. Sigmund Freud, *The Future of an Illusion* (New York: W. W. Norton, 1990).

3. Sigmund Freud, *Civilization and Its Discontents* (London: Penguin, 2002).

4. Henry Miller, "Peace! It's Wonderful!," in *The Cosmological Eye* (New York: New Directions, 1939), 7.

5. Karl Marx and Friedrich Engels, *The Holy Family, or Critique of Critical Critique* (1844), Marxists Internet Archive, https://www.marxists.org/archive/marx/works/1845/holy -family/index.htm.

6. Benedict de Spinoza, *A Spinoza Reader: The "Ethics" and Other Works*, trans. Edwin Curley (Princeton, NJ: Princeton University Press 1994).

7. Thomas à Kempis, *The Imitation of Christ* (London: Penguin Classics, 2013).

8. *Tao Te Ching*, trans. Derek Lin, Taoism.net, http://www .Taoism.net; and *Tao Te Ching: Annotated and Explained* (Nashville, TN: SkyLight Paths, 2006). N.B. Variant spellings.

9. Henry Miller, "An Open Letter to Surrealists Everywhere," in *The Cosmological Eye* (New York: New Directions, 1939), 156.

10. Ibid.

11. Wallace Fowlie, *Letters of Henry Miller and Wallace Fowlie, 1943–1972* (New York: Grove Press, 1972).

12. *Red Emma Speaks: An Emma Goldman Reader*, ed. Alix Kates Shulman (Amherst, NY: Humanity Books, 1998).

13. Henry Miller, *Sexus* (London: Penguin Modern Classics, 2015).

LIKE A FLUID (THE GREAT ROMANTIC)

1. Henry Miller, *On Writing* (New York: New Directions, 1964), 123.

2. Rainer Maria Rilke, *Die Gedichte* (Frankfurt am Main: Insel Verlag, 2006); my rough translation.

3. Henry Miller, *The Colossus of Maroussi* (London: Penguin Classics, 2016), 89.

THE AIR-CONDITIONED NIGHTMARE

1. Henry Miller, *The Colossus of Maroussi* (London: Penguin Classics 2016), 47.

2. Ibid., 199.

3. Henry Miller, *The Air-Conditioned Nightmare* (1945; London, Heinemann, 1962), 11.

4. Harry S. Truman, "Message to the Congress on the State of the Union," 1946, Harry S. Truman Library and Museum, https://www.trumanlibrary.org/whistlestop/tap/11446.htm.

5. Henry Miller, *The Air-Conditioned Nightmare*, 8.

6. Ibid., 138.

7. Ibid., 139.

8. Rodney Jones, "The Assault on the Fields," in *Elegy for the Southern Drawl* (New York: Houghton Mifflin, 1999).

9. Loren Eiseley, *The Immense Journey* (New York: Vintage Books, 1957).

10. William Cobbett, "Rural Ride from Chilworth in Surrey, to Winchester," in *Rural Rides* (London: Penguin Classics, 2001).

11. Text available at Marxists Internet Archive, https://www.marxists.org/archive/morris/works/1882/hopes/chapters/chapter1.htm.

12. Cornel West, *The Cornel West Reader* (New York: Basic Civitas Books, 1999), 208.

13. The four quotations, in the order presented, are from (1) Rachel Carson, *Silent Spring*, 40th anniv. ed. (New York: Houghton Mifflin, 2002), 99; (2) Miller, *The Air-Conditioned Nightmare*, 155; (3) Ibid., 13; (4) Carson, *Silent Spring*, 13.

14. Miller, *The Air-Conditioned Nightmare*, 15.

15. Ibid., 83.

16. Henry Miller, *The Paintings of Henry Miller: Paint as You Like and Die Happy*, ed. Noel Young (Santa Barbara, CA: Capra Press, 1962).

THE TIME OF THE ASSASSINS

1. "Life's own colours deepen, dance, / and become clear again around the Vision under construction" (my translation).

2. "Any man who does not accept the conditions of life sells his soul." Charles Baudelaire, *The Essence of Laughter and Other Essays, Journals, and Letters* (Evanston, IL: Northwestern University Press, 1991).

3. Henry Miller, *The Time of the Assassins* (New York: New Directions, 1962), 29.

4. Carl Jung, *The Collected Works of C. G. Jung: Alchemical Studies* (Princeton, NJ: Princeton University Press 1968).

5. Henry Miller, *The Time of the Assassins*, 48, 49.

6. Ibid.

7. "Geh hinein in dich und baue an deinen Schweren. Dein Schweres soll sein wie ein Haus in dir, wenn du selbst wie ein Land bist, das sich mit den Gezeiten verändert. Gedenke, daß du kein Stern bist: du hast keine Bahn" (Go deep inside yourself and build what's hard. It should be like a house within you, if you yourself are like a land that changes with the tides. Remember, you are not a star, you have no course to follow). R. M. Rilke, "Eine Morgenandacht," quoted in *Rilke: The Inner Sky*, trans. Damion Searls (Boston: David R Godine, 2010).

THE CREATURE WORLD

1. "When I have occasionally set myself to consider the different distractions of men, the pains and perils to which they expose themselves at court or in war, whence arise so many

quarrels, passions, bold and often bad ventures, etc., I have discovered that all the unhappiness of men arises from one single fact, that they cannot stay quietly in their own chamber." Pascal, *Pensées*, trans. A. J. Krailsheimer, reissue ed. (London: Penguin Classics, 1995).

2. Nobelprize.org, https://www.nobelprize.org/nobel_prizes /literature/laureates.

3. Durell to Miller, October 16, 1978, quoted at Cosmo-demonic Telegraph Company: A Henry Miller Blog, http:// cosmotc.blogspot.com/2006/10/millers-campaign-for-nobel -prize.html.

4. "We may see each other again when I receive the Nobel Prize (what a joke!)." Letter to Brassaï, December 1958, in Brassaï, *Henry Miller, Happy Rock*, trans. Jane Marie Todd (Chicago: University of Chicago Press, 2002).

5. "The more we are recognized as winners, the more we know ourselves to be losers. That is why it is rare for the winners of highly coveted and publicized prizes to settle for their titles and retire. Winners, especially celebrated winners, must prove repeatedly they are winners. The script must be played over and over again. Titles must be defended by new contests. No one is ever wealthy enough, honored enough, applauded enough. On the contrary, the visibility of our victories only tightens the grip of the failures in our invisible past." James P. Carse, *Finite and Infinite Games* (New York: Free Press, 1986).

6. Henry Miller, *On Turning Eighty*, Capra Chapbook series, no. 1 (Santa Barbara, CA: Capra Press, 1972).

7. "Oh! nos os sont revêtus d'un nouveau corps amoureux." (Oh! our bones are clothed in an amorous new body.) Arthur Rimbaud, *Poésies, Une saison en enfer, Illuminations*, ed. Louis Forestier (Paris: Gallimard, 1973).

8. Carse, *Finite and Infinite Games*.

9. Tsunetomo Yamamoto, *Hagakure: The Book of the Samurai* (Boulder, CO: Shambhala Publications, 2012).

10. Henry Miller, *The Colossus of Maroussi* (London: Penguin Classics, 2016), 66.

11. Henry Miller, *Tropic of Cancer*, new ed. (London: Harper Perennial, 2005).

12. Robinson Jeffers, *The Collected Poems* (Stanford, CA: Stanford University Press, 2002).

13. Presumably a reference to Rabbi Ben-Ezra, or Abraham ibn Ezra, the twelfth-century poet, scholar, and mathematician, referred to by Fitzgerald in *The Rubaiyat*.

14. Don DeLillo, *Zero K* (New York: Simon and Schuster, 2016), 131.

15. Ferlinghetti, online interview by V. Vale, in *Real Conversations*, 2015, http://www.researchpubs.com/products-page -2/real-conversations-1-excerpt-lawrence-ferlinghetti.

16. DeLillo's Ben-Ezra speaks of "hundreds of millions of people into the future billions who are struggling to find something to eat not once or twice a day but all day every day. He spoke in detail about food systems, weather systems, the loss of forests, the spread of drought, the massive die-offs of birds and ocean life, the levels of carbon dioxide, the lack of drinking water, the waves of virus . . ."

17. DeLillo, *Zero K*, 134–35.

18. Miller, *The Colossus of Maroussi*, 68.

19. Ibid., 35.

20. Henry Miller, *The Books in My Life* (London: Village Press, 1974).

21. Henry Miller, *Mother, China, and the World Beyond* (Santa Barbara, CA: Capra Press, 1977).